John and Charles Wesley

Twayne's English Authors Series

Bertram H. Davis, *Editor*

Florida State University

TEAS 368

JOHN WESLEY
(1703–1791)
From an engraving by William Ridley
after a portrait (c. 1790) by Henry Edridge.
*Courtesy of the Commission on Archives and History,
Central Illinois Conference, United Methodist Church.*

CHARLES WESLEY

CHARLES WESLEY
(1707–1788)
From an engraving by William Tegg after a portrait by Gush.
Courtesy of the Commission on Archives and History,
Central Illinois Conference, United Methodist Church.

John and Charles Wesley

By Samuel J. Rogal

Illinois State University

Twayne Publishers • *Boston*

John and Charles Wesley

Samuel J. Rogal

Copyright © 1983 by G. K. Hall & Company
All Rights Reserved
Published by Twayne Publishers
A Division of G. K. Hall & Company
70 Lincoln Street
Boston, Massachusetts 02111

Book Production by Marne B. Sultz

Book Design by Barbara Anderson

Printed on permanent/durable acid-free
paper and bound in the United States of
America.

Library of Congress Cataloging in Publication Data

Rogal, Samuel J.
  John and Charles Wesley.

  (Twayne's English authors series ; TEAS 368)
  Bibliography: p. 162
  Includes index.
    1. Wesley, John, 1703–1791—Criticism and
interpretation.   2. Wesley, Charles, 1707–1788—Criticism
and interpretation.   I. Title.   II. Series.
PR3763.W5Z85 1983   287'.092'2 [B]   83-8593
ISBN 0–8057–6854–8

For Susan, Geoffrey, and James Paul

"Their faith hath made them whole. And these are of one heart and of one soul. They all love one another, and are knit together in one body and one spirit, as in one faith and one hope of their calling."

John Wesley to Count Zinzendorf
30 October 1738

Contents

About the Author

Samuel J. Rogal teaches undergraduate writing and coordinates the English education program at Illinois State University. In addition to several textbooks on pedagogy and composition, he has authored *A Chronological Outline of British Literature* (Greenwood), *Sisters of Sacred Song: A Bibliographical Survey of Women Hymnodists* (Garland), and *The Children's Jubilee: A Survey of Hymnals for Infants, Youth, and Sunday Schools Published in Great Britain and America* (Greenwood); Scholars' Facsimiles and Reprints published his edition of Isaac Watts's *Reliquiae Juveniles*. His articles on the Wesleys and eighteenth-century hymnody have appeared in *Victorians Institute Journal*, *Journal of Religious Studies*, *Research Studies*, *Eighteenth-Century Life*, *Asbury Seminarian*, *Cresset*, *Studies in Eighteenth-Century Culture*, *Yale Journal of Biology and Medicine*, *Ball State University Forum*, *University of Dayton Review*, *Hymn*, *Milton Quarterly*, *Studies in History and Society*, *Bulletin of the New York Public Library*, *Bulletin of Bibliography*, *Yale University Library Gazette*, *Princeton Seminary Bulletin*, *Methodist History*. Mr. Rogal—who has also taught at Mary Holmes College, State University of New York at Oswego, Iowa State University, and Waynesburg College—holds membership in the Modern Language Association, American Society for Eighteenth-Century Studies, The Hymn Society of America, National Council of Teachers of English, Illinois Association of Teachers of English, and the Historical Society of the Illinois Conference of the United Methodist Church.

Preface

A quarter of a century ago, Professor A. R. Humphreys proclaimed that there "are few greater Englishmen than John Wesley, and to compress his achievements into a paragraph is like trying to see the world in the grain of sand and eternity in an hour." Unfortunately, there have been too many compressed paragraphs on the lives and works of John and Charles Wesley (the latter being the poetic reverberation of his older brother's greatness), too many attempts by literary and social historians and their theological relatives to slap the same generalizations onto the pages of their commentaries and histories. Charles Wesley appears preaching to the colliers at Kingswood, praying for the condemned on their way to Tyburn, writing hymns at the drop of anything that could possibly have been dropped, and pleading with his older brother not to ordain priests for America. John, on the other hand, is pictured as the lonely figure on horseback or in chaise, wending his way through every political division in the island-kingdom, delivering lengthy sermons in the open fields, organizing societies, chastising backsliders, converting the poor, and generally refusing to yield to the presence of widespread opposition against him. With but two or three exceptions, discussion—critical, analytical, historical, theological, hymnological—of the Wesleys has advanced little since the early nineteenth century, principally because Wesleyan biographers and critical commentators have not always been willing or able to view their subjects within the proper context of eighteenth-century British life and thought.

Understandably, the earliest biographers of the Wesleys, as well as the earliest critical commentators upon their poetry and prose, saw their subjects principally as the eighteenth-century founders of a nineteenth-century religious organization. Almost immediately following John Wesley's death at the beginning of March 1791, British Methodism cut its cord from the Church of England and marched quickly into the age of romanticism, revival, and reform as an independent theological and social force, one that was to have a significant effect upon Victorian institutions and attitudes. Thus, such writers as John Hampson, Thomas Coke and Henry Moore, John Whitehead, and Thomas Jackson were in too great a hurry to promote the Wesleys as patriarchs of British Methodism; collations of anecdotes and imperfect recollections became convenient substitutes for the real neoclassical background from which the Wesleys sprung and the classical and preromantic atmospheres in which they lived and worked. Simply, the early writers, most of them churchmen and devoted Methodists, considered John and Charles Wesley their own property; they clung to the image of a modern Moses and Aaron, leading the spiritually impoverished poor of Great Britain away from the cold, detached pyramids of York, Rochester, and Canterbury, exhorting them toward the warmth of City Road Chapel. The best that can be seen of those early attempts appeared, chronologically, between Hampson and Jackson, originating from the pen and the imagination of a "layman." In 1820, Robert Southey, having already done biographical honors to Horatio Nelson, turned to John Wesley and (according to his subtitle) "The Rise and Progress of Methodism." The laureate of England gave the world two volumes of interesting reading and injected some literary respectability into his subject. However, the work contains more than its share of errors—both of fact and interpretation—and its lack of organization tends to confuse the reader.

The purpose of the present study is not merely to disentangle John and Charles Wesley from Southey's apparent disrespect for chronological and thematic order. Nor is there purpose in attempting to "de-Methodize" the efforts of a hard corps of sincere but not always scholarly nineteenth-century and twentieth-century Methodists—joined by psychologists, journalists, novelists, Protestant churchmen, one Roman Catholic, and a future President of the United States—who saw fit to grind out variations upon the same theme: the brothers Wesley as the broad base upon which to pile mountains of statistics relative to the emergence of Methodist circuits, preachers, Bible societies, and Sunday schools. Rather, the aim of this volume is to respond to Mr. Humphreys's not too well concealed plea for more space—space in which to substantiate the notion of the Wesleys' greatness. Again, there exists no argument here against the Wesleys' *Methodist* greatness; there does exist, however, conviction (at least on the part of this writer) that John and

Charles Wesley deserve the label because of what they contributed to the life and to the letters of eighteenth-century Britain. Standing almost alone, the Wesleys sought to counter the pessimism and the antihumanitarianism expressed by the cold projector of Swift's *Modest Proposal;* almost alone, they sought to strip away the darkness manifested by Samuel Johnson's Abyssinian prince, who explicated the notion that, at least for enlightened Englishmen, there was much to be endured but little to be enjoyed; almost alone, they sought to give substance to the shallow Christianity construed by Fielding's quixotic Abraham Adams, the provincial parson who saw the evangelical movement as nothing more than "the detestable doctrine of faith against good works"; almost alone, they set out not only to fill the bellies and the pockets of the impoverished souls among them, but to feed their intellects as well—to teach them the value of learning Greek, French, Hebrew, Milton, electricity, practical medicine, English prosody, and proper pronunciation and gesture.

The point, then, is that during more than fifty years of their maturity, John and Charles Wesley produced a considerable quantity of writing: more than three hundred volumes (including extracts and editions of others' works) can easily be assigned to John; Charles composed in excess of 8900 hymns, in addition to several lengthy, nonliturgical pieces of poetry. Obviously, not all of the elder Wesley's work deserves discussion as serious literature—the grammars, the minutes of and conversations at conferences, the scores of letters focusing strictly upon matters of organization and administration. However, his sermons and religious tracts, the political and historical arguments, certain pedagogical works, and the literary extracts and commentaries are worthy of serious analysis, not only for what they set forth, but for their clear, crisp prose style. As for Charles, the quality of his poetry may not always be at the highest level, but even so he stands as a major figure in the development of English congregational song. He must not be treated as a hack or even as a versifier; he was a serious poet influenced by Bunyan, Milton, Young, Pope, and the Old Testament psalmists. He was admired, among others, by Blake, Coleridge, the Rossettis, Emerson, and Hardy for his ability to inject personal, religious experience into the collective voice of English hymnody. Thus, the present volume focuses upon quality and representativeness in an effort to treat John and Charles Wesley as significant contributors to one of the most vital periods in British literary history.

Samuel J. Rogal

Illinois State University

Chronology

1703   17 June: John Benjamin Wesley born at Epworth to Samuel Wesley and Susanna Annesley Wesley.

1707   18 December: Charles Wesley born at Epworth.

1709   9 February: John Wesley rescued from the fire at Epworth rectory.

1711   12 May: John Wesley nominated for Charterhouse School by the Duke of Buckingham.

1714   28 January: John Wesley admitted to Charterhouse.

1716   Charles Wesley enters Westminster School.

1720   24 June: John Wesley enters Christ Church, Oxford.

1724   John Wesley graduates B.A. from Oxford.

1725   19 September: John Wesley ordained deacon by Dr. John Potter, Bishop of Oxford; 16 October, preaches his first sermon, at South Leigh, Oxfordshire.

1726   Charles Wesley enters Christ Church, Oxford. 14 March: John Wesley elected Fellow of Lincoln College, Oxford; lectures in Greek, philosophy, and logic. April-October: John Wesley assists his father at Epworth and Wroote.

1727   9 February: John Wesley awarded M.A. in religion and natural and moral philosophy. August: John Wesley again leaves Oxford to assist his father at Epworth and Wroote.

1728   John Wesley admitted to priest's orders.

1729   May: Charles Wesley forms the Oxford "Holy Club"; the group is labeled "methodists." November: John Wesley returns to Oxford, presides over Lincoln College public moderations. December: John Wesley joins the Holy Club and assumes its leadership.

1730   Charles Wesley graduates B.A. from Oxford.

1733   12 March: Charles Wesley graduates M.A. from Oxford.

1735   George Whitefield joins the Oxford Holy Club. 25 April: death of Samuel Wesley the elder. 21 October: the Wesleys sail from Gravesend for Georgia aboard the *Simmonds*.

1736   5 February: the Wesleys reach Savannah, Georgia. 11 August: Charles Wesley leaves Georgia, arrives in England on 2 December.

1737   2 December: John Wesley leaves Savannah. John Wesley, *A Collection of Psalms and Hymns*.

1738   1 February: John Wesley returns to England. 21 May: Charles Wesley's evangelical conversion at Bray's, in Little Britain, London. 24 May: "The Aldersgate Experience"—John Wesley's evangelical conversion, Aldersgate Street, London. June: John Wesley visits Count Nicholas von Zinzendorf and the Moravians. John and Charles Wesley, *A Collection of Psalms and Hymns*.

1739   11 November: John Wesley preaches the first sermon at the Foundery, Upper Moorfields, London. John and Charles Wesley, *Hymns and Sacred Poems*.

1740   John and Charles Wesley, *Hymns and Sacred Poems*.

1741   Charles Wesley, *Hymns on God's Everlasting Love*. John Wesley, *A Collection of Psalms and Hymns*.

1742   30 July: death of Susanna Annesley Wesley. John and Charles Wesley, *Hymns and Sacred Poems*.

1743   29 May: opening of West Street Chapel, London.

1745   John Wesley, *Advice to the People Called Methodists*.

1746   John Wesley, *Sermons on Several Occasions* (to 1760).

1747   9 August: John Wesley's first visit to Ireland. John Wesley, *Primitive Physick*.

1748   John Wesley, *English Grammar* and *Latin Grammar*.

1749   8 April: Charles Wesley marries Sarah Gwynne. Charles Wesley, *Hymns and Sacred Poems*. John Wesley, *Directions concerning Pronunciation and Gesture* and edition of *The Christian Library* (50 vols., to 1755).

1750   John Wesley, *A Compendium of Logick*.

1751   John Wesley, *French Grammar* and *Hebrew Grammar*.

1753   John Wesley, *The Complete English Dictionary*.

1755 January: John Wesley, *Notes upon the New Testament.*

1758 John Wesley, *Reasons against a Separation from the Church of England.*

1760 John Wesley, *The Desideratum: or, Electricity made Plain and Useful.*

1761 John Wesley (ed.), *Select Hymns: with Tunes Annext: Designed Chiefly for Use of the People Called Methodists.*

1762 Charles Wesley, *Short Hymns on Select Passages of Holy Scripture.*

1763 Charles Wesley, *Hymns for Children.*

1765 John Wesley, *Explanatory Notes upon the Old Testament*; *Greek Grammar*; and *A Short History of Methodism.*

1766 31 January: John Wesley, *A Plain Account of Christian Perfection.*

1771 Charles Wesley, *An Elegy on the Late Reverend George Whitefield*; *An Epistle to the Reverend George Whitefield.* The Bristol edition of *The Works of the Rev. John Wesley* (32 vols., to 1774).

1773 John Wesley, *A Short Roman History.*

1775 John Wesley, *A Calm Address to Our American Colonies.*

1776 John Wesley, *A Concise History of England*, 4 vols.

1777 John Wesley, *A Calm Address to the Inhabitants of England.*

1778 1 January: first number of John Wesley's *Arminian Magazine.* 1 November: City Road (London) Chapel opened.

1779 John Wesley, *Popery Calmly Considered.*

1780 John and Charles Wesley, *A Collection of Hymns for the Use of the People Called Methodists.*

1781 Death of John Wesley's wife, Molly Vazielle Wesley. John Wesley, *A Concise Ecclesiastical History* (4 vols.).

1785 John Wesley, *A Pocket Hymn Book, for the Use of Christians of All Denominations.*

1788 29 March: death of Charles Wesley. 5 April: Charles Wesley buried at Marylebone, London. John Wesley, *Sermons*, 2nd series (4 vols.).

1790 24 October: last entry in John Wesley's journal. March: John Wesley, *Hymns for Children* (selected from Charles Wesley's *Hymns for Children*). John Wesley's last major publication, *The New Testament, with an Analysis of the Several Books and Chapters*.

1791 24 February: John Wesley's last piece of writing—a letter of encouragement to William Wilberforce. 2 March: death of John Wesley, at 10:00 A.M. 9 March: John Wesley buried at City Road, London.

Chapter One
Family and Background

A popular genealogical exercise of nineteenth-century Wesleyan biographers and historians of Methodism was to trace the Wesley family as far back as 1339, to one Baron William de Wellesley and his second son, Sir Richard, and to carry it forward to no less a figure than Arthur Wellesley, Duke of Wellington.[1] For the purpose of this rather brief biographical treatment, however, we need retreat no farther than the late sixteenth century, when Sir Herbert Westley,[2] of Westleigh in Devonshire, married Elizabeth de Wellesley of Dangan, Ireland. From that union came forth the paternal great-grandfather of John and Charles Wesley, Bartholomew Westley—a student of medicine and divinity at Oxford and, from 1640 to 1661, rector of Charmouth and Catherston, Dorset. He married the daughter of Sir Henry Colley of Kildare, who bore him one son, John. In 1661, while restoration of the monarchy and the Established Church still stood as the prominent activity, Bartholomew, obviously because of his Puritan and anti-royalist sympathies, found himself ejected from his living; he spent the remaining ten years of his life practicing medicine and Nonconformity.

The lone son, John Westley, followed upon the path of his father's Nonconformity. After specializing in oriental languages at New Inn Hall, Oxford, he joined a separatist church at Weymouth, eventually became its preacher, and then formed another such congregation at nearby Radipole. Although never having prepared for or received episcopal ordination, John Westley, in May 1658, was appointed, by the Triers,[3] vicar of Winterborn-Whitechurch, Dorset, a position from which he was removed in 1662, almost a year after his father's ejection. Thus, the paternal grandfather of John and Charles Wesley spent his remaining years living and preaching among a variety of Dissenting sects, including Baptists, Quakers, and Independents (referred to now as Congregationalists) in and around Weymouth, Taunton, Bridgewater, Preston, Ilminster, and Poole. That he was arrested and thrown into the jails of Dorchester and Poole on at least four occasions testifies to the zeal with which he carried on his ministry, as well as to the degree to which he irritated local representatives of an overly sensitive Establishment and its forms of religious "toleration."[4]

Sometime during late 1658 or early 1659, John Westley married a Miss White, who, although then an orphan, had come from noteworthy stock. Her uncle, Thomas Fuller, authored more than a dozen significant tracts in church history, the most useful being *The Church History of Britain from the Birth of Christ to 1648* (1655). John White, the girl's father, rector of Trinity Church, Dorchester, and known as "The Patriarch of Dorchester," published a score of sermons and biblical commentaries—particularly a *Commentary on the First Three Chapters of Genesis* (pub. 1656). According to Edward Everett of Massachusetts, "John White never set foot upon the soil of Massachusetts, but he was the most efficient promoter of the undertaking which resulted not only in the settlement of our ancient town [Dorchester, Massachusetts], but of the colony."[5] The marriage undoubtedly would have been a happy one had it not been for Westley's need to evade the enforcers of the Clarendon Code; he was, at his death, only forty-two years old, leaving his widow and numerous children. Of the latter, only the names of four have survived: Matthew became a successful London physician; Samuel altered both the family denominational direction and the spelling of the family name; of Timothy and Elizabeth, nothing can or need be said. Finally, we may note that John Westley's widow survived, for the major portion of the thirty-two years following her husband's death, on allowances of £10 per year received from her sons.

There exists hardly the slightest doubt that had not Samuel Wesley the elder been partly responsible for bringing three noteworthy sons into the world, both his name and his literary labors would have remained as obscure as the two hamlets in Lincolnshire where he was forced to act out his role as agent of the Church of England. However, the details of his early career, his marriage, the ministries at Epworth and Wroote, and his poetry are essential parts to the overall histories of his offspring; in addition, those details cast light on the specific problems confronting the rural English clergyman of the late seventeenth and early eighteenth centuries.

As the son of a Nonconformist, the young Samuel Westley found only a single avenue toward formal education open to him. He began as a student of Henry Dolling at the Free School, Dorchester, after which the Independents dispatched him, in March 1678, to study with the learned Theophilus Gale, former fellow of Magdalen College, Oxford. Unfortunately, before the newest student could reach the steps of his school in the Holborn section of London, Gale died; Westley then settled upon Edward Veal's academy in Stepney. After two years there he moved on to Newington Green, London, to study with Charles Morton,[6] there finding himself in company with at least three young men who would later establish themselves in the world of letters: the sermon rhetorician Timothy Cruso, the novelist and pamphleteer Daniel Defoe,[7] and the master funeral sermonizer Rev. John Shower. Although the youth lived during this period with his mother and an old aunt, he received financial support from two sources: £30 from the Dorchester Nonconformists and an additional £10 yearly from Dr. John Owen, Dean of Christ Church and Vice Chancellor of Oxford under Cromwell. More recently leader of a congregation of Calvinist Dissenters in Leadenhall Street, London, Owen had written over eighty theological tracts and biblical commentaries, sixty-seven of which were published between 1642 and 1682.[8]

Owen's interest in the Westleys had begun in the 1650s with John Westley's studies in oriental languages at New Inn Hall, Oxford; the scholar-cleric then noticed young Samuel's witty verse and generally active mind in the pursuit of his studies, and he therefore encouraged him (principally with the annual gift of £10) to consider theology and critical scholarship, as well as to develop the immature attacks and lampoons against church and state begun at Morton's academy. Actually, the largest portion of those dabblings in rhyme were directed against Rev. Thomas Doolittle, a Presbyterian divine and author, whose academy stood as a rival to that of Charles Morton. At any rate, while in the midst of those poetical barbs, the very critical and analytical mind that had so attracted Dr. Owen's attention began to examine both sides of the current political and theological divisions; in the end, before he reached age twenty-one, Samuel Westley determined to abandon Nonconformity and to go so far as to prepare himself for entrance and then officership in the very church from which his family had been for so long estranged. In August 1683, he entered Exeter College, Oxford, as a *Pauper Scholaris,* where his poverty forced him to employ his pen for very practical purposes.[9] As a *servitor*—one who received free lodging and most of his board, as well as an exemption from lecture fees—young Westley[10] stood at the call of more affluent and less industrious classmates, for whom he prepared exercises and gave tutorial instruction. He soon found, however, a more satisfactory source for funds.

In all probability, Samuel Wesley established contact with the eccentric bookseller and publisher, John Dunton, while Wesley was in attendance at Charles Morton's academy. Ironically, the first item published after Dunton opened his London shop turned out to be *The Lord's Last Sufferings,* by Thomas Doolittle, the very rival of Morton against whom young Wesley had been directing his juvenile lampoons; the London printer's third publication, a funeral sermon, came from John Shower, Wesley's classmate at the Newington Green academy.[11] Finally, there is reason to believe that Wesley attended, on 3 August 1682, Dunton's marriage to Elizabeth Annesley, whose thirteen-year-old sister would become, in eight years, his own wife.[12] Dunton's early successes with the tracts and sermons of Dissenters enabled him to expand his efforts; in 1685, he published *Maggots; or, Poems on Several Subjects, never before handled. By a Scholar,* dedicated to Henry Dolling of the grammar school in Dorchester. The "Scholar" was Samuel Wesley, then in his second year at Exeter; the general quality of the volume may immediately be determined by a glance at the frontispiece, a combination drawing and caricature portrait of the poet seated at his desk, crowned with laurel, a maggot upon his forehead.[13] Beneath the picture are the lines,

> In's own defence the author writes,
> Because when this foul maggot bites
>   he ne'er can rest in quiet,
> Which makes him make so sad a face,
> He'd beg your worship on your grace
>   Unsight, unseen by it.

If the front matter and the juvenilia that followed were not enough to bring about the demise of the volume, contemporary economics mercifully intervened; the depression of 1685, brought on principally by the Duke of Monmouth's insurrection, forced John Dunton to close his shop at the Black Raven, Prince's Street, and strike out for Puritan New England, there to replenish his depleted coffers.

The relationship between Samuel Wesley and John Dunton did not, however, end with the publication of *Maggots*. By November 1686, the printer and bookseller was back in business (opposite the Poultry Compter, London), and an apparent upward turn in his fortunes allowed him to embark upon certain literary projects of his own. Chief among those was the *Athenian Mercury* (initially the *Athenian Gazette)*, a penny journal issued weekly from 17 March 1690 until 14 June 1697. The plan for the periodical called for readers to submit questions on science, literature, and philosophy; the answers were serious enough, but contained sufficient "lightness" to remain interesting and diverting. In other words, Dunton sought and apparently found the very reading public that contributed, twenty years later, to the success of the *Tatler* and the *Spectator;* as did Addison and Steele, the London bookseller sought the intelligent, but not necessarily the erudite, and he struggled hard to avoid controversy and to satisfy curiosity. Since Dunton's own intellectual and educational shortcomings would not allow him to respond satisfactorily to all questions, he employed specialists to assist him with his project; to that end, he turned early to Samuel Wesley and Richard Sault, as well as to John Norris.[14] Wesley, at this point, had only begun his clerical and literary career, but Dunton called upon him to provide answers to most of the theological questions and to a small portion of the philosophical queries. Although then situated some distance from the center of British learning and literary activity, Samuel Wesley, through his experiences with the *Athenian Mercury,* demonstrated that he could respond easily and intelligently to the needs of a growing reading audience. Unfortunately, he never could turn the opportunity offered through Dunton's successful journalistic adventure to his own advantage in that area. In 1692, Wesley did some hack work for Dunton, compiling *The Young Student's Library*—synopses of eighty-nine works in divinity, history, and science; the project added to the bookseller's purse, but contributed nothing to its editor's fame or fortune.

The short pieces for Dunton's *Athenian Mercury* may well have been the highlight of Samuel Wesley's literary career, for nothing that he wrote before or after them attracted much attention, at least in literary circles. In June 1688, he contributed some verse to *Strenae Natalitiae Academiae Oxoniensis,* a volume dedicated to James Francis Edward, the only son born to James II and Mary of Modena;[15] five years later, on 13 July 1693, appeared *The Life of Our Blessed Lord and Saviour Jesus Christ,* an heroic poem in ten books, illustrated, annotated, dedicated to Queen Mary, and containing a prefatory essay on heroic poetry. The piece is tedious, lengthy, and often beyond belief, as the poet vainly strives to relate matters of fundamental theological concern to contemporary political issues; he succeeds only in making readers appreciate more the genius of Milton and Dryden. "Only a true-blue Whig," wrote H. N. Fairchild, "would bring William III and [the battle of] the Boyne into an account of the Crucifixion."[16] As luck would have it, Mary died on 28 December 1694, which meant that the rector of South Ormsby, Lincolnshire, had little else to show for his giant effort but an epic poem of questionable quality (albeit one that went through several editions). At the outset of 1695, Wesley joined the long line of versifiers who determined to mourn William III's queen; toward the end of the century, he published *The Pious Communicant Rightly Prepar'd* (London: For C. Harper at the Flower de Luce in Fleet Street, 1699), a discourse on the sacrament and baptism. In his *Epistle to a Friend concerning Poetry* (London: C. Harper, 1700), he set forth an unconvincing defense of Sir Richard Blackmore, physician to Queen Anne and the author of *The Creation,* while criticizing those poets whose works, according to his standards, lacked both religious and moral insight.

Aside from some miscellaneous verse and prose tracts on the education of Dissenters (1702–1705), only two other pieces deserve notice. Obviously not content to have published one epic poem that he propped up with a large number of illustrations, Samuel Wesley furnished the world with yet another biblical extravaganza and dedicated it to Queen Anne: *The History of the Old and New Testament in Verse; with 330 Sculptures. In Three Volumes.* Although the work, like at least a dozen other heavily laden volumes published during the period, managed to survive through several editions, its reputation was secured for the wrong reasons and established in the wrong places. For example, in Pope's *Dunciad Variorum,* the Queen of Dulness casts an eye upon her prince, sitting at his desk and surrounded by "much learned lumber":

> Volumes, whose size the space exactly fill'd;
> Or which fond authors were so good to gild;
> Or where, by sculpture made for ever known,
> The page admires new beauties, not its own. (I, 111–20)[17]

Nearly a quarter-century earlier, Swift had taken care of the matter in more succinct terms when, in his *Battel of the Books* (1704), "Homer slew W-sl-y with a kick of his heel. . . ."[18]

The critical guns were silent, however, when the second of the two projects appeared before the public, principally because the rector from Lincolnshire could no longer be numbered among the living! Almost from the beginning of his appointment to Epworth rectory, Wesley had been working, somewhat spasmodically, upon a treatise on the Book of Job. The exact length of time he had devoted to that labor is difficult to determine, for the materials collected for the manuscript—the Hebrew, Greek, Latin, and English versions of Job—perished in 1709 when the rector's unruly parishioners burned his house to the ground. Undaunted, even under siege by gout and palsy, he employed amanuenses, one being his son John, and printed proposals in 1729. On 4 March 1730, Pope devoted an entire letter to Swift, "to do and say nothing but recommend to you, as a clergyman, and a charitable one, a pious and good work, and for a good and honest man," hoping that "you will approve his prose more than you formerly could his poetry."[19] One can only speculate as to whether Pope had ever cast his eyes upon Wesley's *Dissertationes in Librum Jobi;* in all probability, his plea to Swift was occasioned by friendship with and some favors owed to Samuel Wesley the younger, sympathy for the old rector's infirmed and impoverished condition, or perhaps a prick of conscience from having alluded to the elder Wesley in one of the *Dunciad* versions. A month later, 9 April 1730, Pope again addressed the matter to Swift: "Lord Oxford lately wrote to you on behalf of a very valuable clergyman's father's book. I wish you could promote it, but expect little from poor Ireland by your accounts of it." In his reply of 2 May, Swift confessed that "I writ to my Lord Oxford the other day, and told him sincerely that I had not credit to get one subscriber for Mr. Wesley except myself."[20] When the fifty-three dissertations finally appeared in 1735, principally through the efforts of John and Samuel Wesley the younger, they very much resembled the grandiosity of *The Life of Christ* and *The History of the Old and New Testament:* the front matter consisting of a portrait of the former rector of Epworth and Wroote, in splendid dress and holding a scepter, followed by a number of highly ornamented plates and a dedication to Queen Caroline.

On Sunday, 12 October 1735, nine days before he sailed for Georgia, John Wesley delivered his father's book to Caroline and enjoyed, in his phrase, "many good words and smiles." An early biographer of Methodism's founder and leader stated that his subject reported that on the occasion of the formal presentation, the queen was enjoying a romp with her maids of honor. She gave Wesley an audience, however, received his father's *Dissertationes,* and remarked, "It is very prettily bound." She quickly placed it, without further examination, on the window ledge, smiled and spoke several words, then returned to her sport.[21] Thus, the literary career of Samuel Wesley the elder had come to rest, fittingly enough, amidst the useless diversion of a royal garden. Like the man, the prose and the poetry contained ample piety; like the man, however, neither really achieved anything approaching significance or even adequate recognition.

Indeed, the path from Oxford which Samuel Wesley trod after becoming, on 19 June 1688, Bachelor of Arts had seemed lined with ample *promise* of success. Thomas Sprat ordained him deacon at Bromley on 7 August; Henry Compton ordained him priest at St. Andrew's, Holborn, on 24 February 1690. Following some months at sea as chaplain aboard a man-of-war, he obtained a curacy in London (worth £30 per year), married and moved to South Ormsby, Lincolnshire, as rector at £50 per annum. There he remained for five years before being appointed rector of Epworth, Lincolnshire, in 1695, a living worth £200. Unfortunately, he was £150 in debt when he arrived; the addition, in 1721, of the rectory at Wroote, five miles from Epworth, came too late and proved too little to ease his financial problems. In fact, it merely broadened his responsibility to the point where he could not handle the two posts. Yet he never really paid that much attention to finances; two prison terms, two fires, two crop failures, and an unruly mob for parishioners failed to shake his poetic temperament or to cast even a shadow over the golden image he had conjured for himself as the anointed "Poet of the Isle of Axholme."[22] Arguments with his wife resulted in a series of eventual reconciliations which, in turn, resulted in a series of children—nineteen in all between 1691 and 1710, ten of whom survived infancy. On 4 June 1731, Samuel Wesley was thrown from a wagon; for the next four years he suffered from the effects of his injuries, compounded by recurring attacks of gout. Mercifully, he died on 25 April 1735, thus bringing to conclusion more than four decades of struggle and failure.

Despite the dreams of Samuel Wesley—political, poetical, and theological—that never materialized, despite his bumbling and his incompetence, his family survived Epworth rectory. It survived because his wife, Susanna, provided more than enough strength to compensate for his weakness. As did her husband, she came from Nonconformity, the twenty-fifth child of Dr. Samuel Annesley, nephew of the first Earl of Anglesea, pastor of a Nonconformist church in Little St. Helen's, Bishopsgate, London, and the so-called "St. Paul of the Nonconformists." Her mother, Annesley's second wife, was the daughter of John White, the Puritan lawyer and Member of Parliament for Southwark in 1640. In 1682, the year of her sister's marriage to John Dunton, the thirteen-year-old Susanna determined to reject her father's religious dissent and to cast her theological lot with the Established Church. Despite the religious liberty achieved at an early age, she remained anchored to her father's household until her marriage to the recently ordained Samuel Wesley; then she settled into (or, more than likely, she became resigned to) her new life, raising her husband's children, enduring her husband's hardships and misfortunes, and bearing up under his idiosyncracies.

On 11 October 1709, the year that saw the destruction by fire of Epworth rectory and periodic visits of the rector to London, Susanna Wesley wrote to her eldest son, Samuel: "There is nothing I now desire to live for, but to do some small service to my children: that, as I have brought them into the world, I may, if it please God, be an instrument of doing good to their souls."[23] Thus we see a summary of the woman's real and total contribution to history, the contribution filtered through the ancient institution of motherhood. If British Methodism sprang from the formation, in 1729, of the Oxford Holy Club, its seeds were planted by Susanna Wesley at Epworth rectory during the opening decade of the eighteenth century. She alone dressed and undressed her infants and changed their clothes, all at fixed hours of the day. She alone rocked each child to sleep at a specified hour. When an infant Wesley became old enough to sit and to eat without assistance, she included that child within the circle of the family table; there the child asked for and ate everything that the mother provided. She prohibited any drinking or eating between meals. At Epworth rectory, evening prayers, at 6:00 P.M., preceded dinner, which took less than one hour. At 7:00, she prepared each child for bed, the youngest first; by 8:00, all Wesley children lay tucked beneath their blankets.

In assuming responsibility for educating her children—a responsibility ceded to her by virtue of the rector's attentiveness to more esoteric matters—Susanna Wesley relied even more heavily upon method. In a letter to her son John, written on 24 July 1732, ten years before her death, she explicated the principles upon which she maintained order in a world constantly under siege by the harbingers of chaos. Her thesis focused upon pure obedience: "I insist upon conquering the will of children . . . because this is the only strong and rational foundation of a religious education, without which both precept and example will be ineffectual. But when this is thoroughly done, then a child is capable of being governed by the reason and piety of its parents, till its own understanding comes to maturity and the principles of religion have taken root in the mind."[24] The thesis then yielded eight bylaws that formed the frame for her method: (1) a full confession of a fault, with a promise to correct it—eliminating lying and needless beating; (2) no sinful act to pass without punishment; (3) no child to be beaten twice for the same fault; (4) a significant act of obedience to be recognized and sometimes even rewarded; (5) an intention toward obedience, even if the performance was not as well as it should have been, to be accepted and encouraged; (6) respect for the privacy and property of others; (7) promises to be strictly enforced and observed; (8) no girl to be put to work (e.g. sewing) before she could read.[25]

The specifics in support of the bylaws took the form of instruction in prayer, blessing by signs, collects, Catechism, and Scripture; when a child reached the age of five, the mother-tutor turned her attention to matters practical: the alphabet, spelling, reading, and mathematics. However, her most noteworthy practice, one that became a fixture within the regimen of her most famous offspring, concerned the allotted time given to private discussion with each child: "I take," she wrote to her husband in early 1712, "such a proportion of time as I can spare every night to discourse with each child apart. On Monday I talk with Molly; on Tuesday with Hetty; Wednesday with Nancy; Thursday with Jacky [John]; Friday with Patty; Saturday with Charles; and with Emily and Suky together on Sunday."[26] Thus did Susanna Wesley both cope with and escape from the disorder surrounding the "Poet of the Isle of Axholme."

She established her own island, her own independent state, wherein she reigned, alone and absolute, preparing daughters to marry Anglican clergymen and sons to become Anglican bishops. She left Samuel Wesley the elder to soar among the clouds of his own insignificance.

Chapter Two

The Education of John and Charles Wesley

To examine eighteenth-century Wesleyan Methodism within the framework of theological and sociological respectability that it deserves, rather than to view it as a series of outdoor gatherings dedicated to religious enthusiasm that lasted for over fifty years, we really need to begin with the *formal* education of its founders. Once John and Charles Wesley left the protection of their self-styled "obedience" clinic, they passed on from the formation of their sense of discipline to the development of their intellects. They advanced, as it were, from the birch to the books, at which point they would learn to assimilate and then react to ideas conceived in the minds of intellectual superiors. Susanna Wesley simply placed into the compartments of their minds the most elementary prescriptions related to the most basic academic disciplines; Charterhouse, Westminster School, and Christ Church, Oxford, would train them to digest ideas, to create ideas, and to convey ideas—their own as well as those of others. They would learn to communicate with persons at almost every level on the elevator of human intellect.

Although John Wesley's entrance to the Charterhouse, London, dates from 28 January 1714,[1] his nomination to that ancient institution came more than two years earlier, on 12 May 1711. Once again, the thin political connections of Samuel Wesley the elder functioned as the vehicle that would launch the poor rector's sons into the world. During his London residence, the father of the Wesleys had come in contact with John Sheffield, first Duke of Buckingham and Normanby, Lord Chamberlain, and author of *An Essay on Satire* and several other poems of only average quality. After the fire at Epworth rectory in 1703, Sheffield sent the elder Wesley £26 17s. and 6d.;[2] the nomination of the latter's son, to be educated on the foundation (free from fees), came as merely one more instance of the duke's benevolence.

The monastery based on the system of La Grande Chartreuse (*Charterhouse* is simply a corruption of the French term) dates to 1371; the actual founding of the school by Thomas Sutton occurred on 3 October 1614. Thus, when John Wesley entered in January 1714, at age ten and a half, the institution was entering the second century of its existence, with approximately one hundred scholars: sixty or so from London who paid fees and between forty and fifty-four boys on foundation grants.[3] During Wesley's tenure at the school, three persons directed his education, all of whom had some degree of influence upon his future ideas, reactions, and practices. We must understand first, however, that the Charterhouse was really two institutions—the school and the adjoining pensioners' hospital—under the direction of a master, who served as governor of the school and head of the hospital. In 1714, the position had been held, since 1685, by Thomas Burnet, whose fame had been secured, between 1681 and 1689, with the publication of *The Sacred Theory of the Earth*,[4] a multi-volume work on terrestrial revolutions, noted more for the writer's style than for its substance. More directly, two individuals emerged as John Wesley's tutors at Charterhouse: Thomas Walker, the principal schoolmaster, and Andrew Tooke, usher, who succeeded Walker as master.

Despite its age and the high quality of education offered there, Charterhouse was not the most prestigious of English schools. Thus, aside from an occasional Addison, Steele, Wesley, or (much later) William Thackeray, all of whom came from rather "common" stock, the rolls of its scholars do not make for interesting reading or even for the recalling of significant details or experiences. Although Wesley held a strong attachment to the school, he remained vague on the specifics of his training there. He visited it regularly, especially after having been away from London for any length, finding a room for meditation and writing, or simply wandering about the grounds. There remains little doubt that because of his early education and his association with persons of learning, John Wesley had to fight hard to control his preference for the yards of an English public school over the open fields during a gathering of rustic Methodists. Such a statement may appear to be heretical, especially when placed beside the reaction of one of the most respected biographers of the Methodist leader, who lamented, "Terrible is the danger when a child leaves a pious home for a public school. John Wesley entered the Charterhouse a saint, and left it a sinner."[5] He may well have, at some point along the highway from Epworth to London, acquired a halo and a pair of wings for protection against the sins of Charterhouse School. Nevertheless, the young man who, on the eve of his entrance to Christ Church, Oxford, sat reading and transcribing Hebrew, had the makings of a competent scholar—competent according to the standards of any age.

By the time Charles Wesley found himself ready to emerge from Epworth rectory, the issue of his schooling had been fairly well settled. Samuel Wesley the younger had already established himself as an usher at Westminster School; there seemed no reason why the thirteen-year-old Charles could not enter that institution and live with Samuel and Ursula Wesley. He did exactly that, remaining under his brother's care from 1716 to 1721, when, after his selection as a king's scholar, he moved to St. Peter's College, that part of the school reserved for king's scholars, where they received room and board without charge. The coveted honor, based upon academic competition, assured the recipient entrance either to Christ Church, Oxford, or Trinity College, Cambridge. A further prize earned by Charles Wesley was that of *Captain* of Westminster School; that award came to him in 1725 by virtue of his being at the head of the list of king's scholars.

It is indeed interesting to note, within the total context of eighteenth-century British life, that the sensitive poet of Methodism, who began his own evangelical mission among the prisoners of Newgate, the condemned at Tyburn, and the colliers of Kingswood, rose out of an educational system directed toward meeting the intellectual needs of the wealthy and the social elite. In other words, during Charles Wesley's tenure, Westminster was the school of and for the British aristocracy, the responsibility for that reputation having been placed directly upon the headmaster, Dr. Robert Freind, who had served as master when Samuel Wesley the younger attended the school. Freind came to Westminster in 1680 as a scholar on the foundation; in 1686, he entered Christ Church, where he ultimately received the degrees of B.A., M.A., B.D., and D.D. Returning to Westminster in 1698 as a proctor, he advanced to undermaster in 1699 and then to headmaster in 1711; in 1711 he also attained the position as rector of Witney, Oxfordshire.

During the twenty-two years of his headmastership, Freind combined an astute social awareness with a respectable publication record to create an air of learning and sophistication throughout Westminster School. He knew Swift and Atterbury intimately, but managed to keep the proper political distance; he had written the proper poems and prose pieces for the right occasions. The headmaster owned a large house situated next to the school; here, about eighty sons of the nobility and gentry resided and took meals, and were overseen by a matron and attended by an usher and a staff of servants. The poor scholars, on the other hand, resided in school dormitory rooms, where they arose at 5:00 A.M. to make their beds and to sweep their rooms before beginning lessons. However, pupils of both social classes wrestled with the same classical curriculum: intensive studies in Greek and Latin grammar; close readings of Virgil, Horace, Ovid, Terence, Cicero, and Livy; laborious exercises in the modes of classical rhetoric. The discipline acquired by Charles Wesley at Epworth rectory prepared him to cope with the rigors of the curriculum styled generations before by Richard Busby and implemented with equal prescriptiveness by Robert Freind; in fact, the assignments and the exercises established the very roots that would later produce a learned poetical style.

The extent to which young Charles Wesley developed as a child of the Establishment, the extent to which he formed distinct social and intellectual habits, may be viewed and understood within the context of his associations at Westminster School. A brief look at several of his classmates reveals individuals from various backgrounds who rose to positions of prominence within the traditional institutions that had controlled Britain in past ages and would continue to control the island-kingdom for the next two centuries: Gerard Andrewes, vicar of Syston and St. Nicholas, Leicester, and master of the Leicester Grammar School; Sir Thomas Clarke (1703–1764), wealthy lawyer, Master of the Rolls, and a Fellow of the Royal Society; William Murray, Lord Mansfield (1704–1793), attorney-general, chief justice of the King's Bench, one of the principal targets of the *Letters of Junius* (1772), and a neighbor of Charles Wesley in the Marylebone section of London; Thomas Newton, D.D. (1704–1782), Bishop of Bristol, who produced a two-volume edition of Milton's *Paradise Lost* and an edition of *Paradise Regained*; James Johnson, the individual who won out over Samuel Wesley the younger for the undermastership of Westminster and who later became Bishop of Worcester; Richard Robinson, Baron Rokeby, prebendary of York, Archbishop of Armagh, Dean of Christ Church, Dublin, and founder of the Armagh Observatory; Andrew Stone, one of the most influential figures in the Hanoverian court who, in addition to functioning as a counselor and confidant, served as Secretary of State to Barbados, Commissioner of Trade and Plantations, and treasurer to Queen Charlotte Sophia; George Stone, brother of Andrew (the latter being partly responsible for his rapid rise in the Church), who succeeded Richard Robinson as Archbishop of Armagh and became known as the dictator of that Irish county.

There was never any doubt that John and Charles Wesley would follow their elder brother Samuel to Christ Church, Oxford, and then to ordination by the Church of England. The latter had been available to assist his brothers during their respective terms at Charterhouse and Westminster School. However, from London to Christ Church, Samuel Wesley the younger could forward only financial help and counsel by correspondence. First John, then Charles, would be left to his own moral and intellectual resources, albeit resources planted and nurtured at their mother's home-style academy and cultivated by serious and competent schoolmasters. The question, then, became not so much whether the Wesleys could survive at Oxford, but whether the seeds of Epworth and the plantings of Charterhouse and Westminster would yield, by the banks of the River Isis, a worthwhile harvest.

Unlike a majority of his predecessors and classmates, seventeen-year-old Jack Wesley did not gawk at the sights or become exhilarated by the sounds of Oxford. He had come, as Susanna Wesley hoped he would, to prepare himself for ordination as a priest in the Church of England; he had come, as his father and elder brother hoped he would, to improve his knowledge of critical learning and ancient and classical languages and literatures; perhaps, in the process, he would develop competence as a poet. The preparation, the improvement, the development began with George Wigan, John Wesley's first tutor at Oxford, who had received his earliest training at Westminster School as a scholar of Dr. Robert Freind; he then moved on to Christ Church, and ultimately became principal of New Inn Hall. His contemporaries and colleagues described Wigan as a disciplinarian and a sober, studious, and learned man whose knowledge of Hebrew stood him in good stead for projects on the Septuagint.[6] On 23 December 1723, Wesley informed his mother that Wigan "had resigned his pupils and was retired into the country to one of his livings" *(Letters,* 1:5). That left his education in the hands of Rev. Henry Sherman, whose kindness toward his pupil (and, later, toward his younger brother Charles) made him a personal friend as well as tutor, one who dispensed fatherly advice from one packet and bound books in the other. On 10 March 1725, Wesley composed a list of seventeen of his closest confidants at Oxford; he placed the name of Rev. Sherman at the top *(Journal,* 1:77).

It is dangerous to assume that John Wesley entered Christ Church as a young, self-styled moralist who refused to examine life beyond the pages of his Greek and Latin texts. To the contrary, he enjoyed the good moments; he apparently had sufficient taste and wit to mix easily with his fellow undergraduates, although he was restricted somewhat by a generally frail physical condition. Nonetheless, on 5 December 1726, he informed Samuel Wesley the younger that "Leisure and I have taken leave of one another; I propose to be busy as long as I live . . ." *(Letters,* 1:34). Such a decision was neither sudden nor guilt-ridden; it resulted from a program of careful reading, analysis, and inquiry begun, most probably, toward the end of his tenure as an undergraduate at Christ Church.

Early letters to his mother and to his brother Samuel reveal that young John Wesley possessed an awareness of a wide variety of works, from the literary to the popular, from the classics to his own contemporaries. He knew the *Spectator* papers of Addison and Steele, and he had more than passing familiarity with Dr. George Cheyne's very practical *Essay of Health and Long Life.* Henry Sherman, his tutor, presented him, on December 1724, with Edward Fairfax's translation of Torquato Tasso's *Jerusalem Delivered,* in which the lovers prepare to face martyrdom to save the Christian inhabitants of the beleaguered Holy City. However, the work that was to begin forming the man of devotion and purpose crossed his path four months prior to his ordination as deacon of the Church of England. He informed his mother, on 28 May 1725, that he had read (by way of translation)[7] *De Imitatione Christi* of Thomas à Kempis, the mid-fifteenth-century tract in which the Augustinian monk traced the gradual progress of the soul to Christian perfection, its detachment from the world, and its eventual union with God. The reactions of the young Oxford scholar to that work are quite detailed in letters to Susanna Wesley, who continued to function as his counselor *in absentia*; he summarized them in his journals thirteen years later, following his religious conversion:

> . . .the providence of God directing me to Kempis's *Christian Pattern*, I began to see that true religion was seated in the heart, and that God's law extended to all our thoughts as well as words and actions. I was, however, very angry with Kempis for being too strict; though I read him only in Dean Stanhope's translation. Yet I had frequently much sensible comfort in reading him, as I was an utter stranger to him before; . . . I began to alter the whole form of my conversation, and to set in earnest upon a new life. I set apart an hour or two a day for religious retirement. I communicated every week. I watched against all sin, whether in word or deed. I began to aim at, and pray for, inward holiness. So that now, "doing so much, and living so good a life," I decided not but I was a good Christian.   (*Journal*, 1:466–67)

Hard upon the heels of Thomas à Kempis, in that same year of 1725, John Wesley came across Jeremy Taylor's two tracts, *Holy Living* (1650) and *Holy Dying* (1651), from which he learned the values of humility, repentance, and practical discipline. In George Berkeley's *Three Dialogues between Hylas and Philonus* (1713), he came to grips with the broad philosophical issues related to skepticism, matter, contradiction, and conception; in the two-volume *A Body of Divinity* (1718–1720), by Richard Fiddes, he wrestled with a definition of faith on purely rational grounds. With all of the preceding to ponder, Wesley still found the time to peruse sermons by Francis Atterbury and Bishop Benjamin Hoadly concerning the Bangorian Controversy and to digest poems by George Herbert and Thomas Parnell.

The works that most influenced Wesley during the period of his early twenties came from the pen of William Law, then tutor to Edward Gibbon the elder's son, the father of the noted historian. In 1726, Law published the first of his treatises on practical morality, *A Practical Treatise on Christian Perfection*; three years later, he produced the second piece, the popular *Serious Call to a Devout and Holy Life*, wherein he explained the life of a single-hearted devotion to the literal precepts of the Gospel. Although Wesley did not agree with every one of Law's qualifications necessary for the devout and holy life, by his own admission "they convinced me more than ever of the exceeding height and breadth and depth of the law of God. The light flowed in so mightily upon my soul, that everything appeared in a new view. I cried out to God for help, and resolved not to prolong the time of obeying Him as I had never done before. And by my continued endeavours to keep His whole law, inward and outward, to the utmost of my power, I was persuaded that I should be accepted of Him, and that I was even then in a state of salvation" *(Journal,* 1:467). Indeed, it was William Law who first sent the Wesleys, William Morgan, and other members of the Oxford Holy Club beyond the walls of Oxford University and into the prisons and among the poor and the sick of the town. Two prose tracts written as guides for traditional Christians and Anglican churchmen became, then, the preamble to eighteenth-century British Methodism.

The next phase in the education of John Wesley presented itself in the form of a fellowship at Lincoln College, Oxford, an award reserved for those natives of Lincolnshire. The one vacant fellowship had been created by the resignation, on 3 May 1725, of John Thorold; the officers of Lincoln College, reacting to the last gasp of influence left in the rector of Epworth and partly to slight pressure from Samuel Wesley the younger, had kept the position vacant for ten and a half months. Then, on 17 March 1726, John Wesley was elected Fellow of Lincoln College;[8] with the exception of the two leaves of absence spent at Epworth and Wroote assisting his father, he would remain there until his departure for the Georgia colony in October 1735. That he was pleased with Lincoln College became evident within the initial month of residence. "As far as I have observed," he wrote to his brother Samuel on 4 April, "I never knew a college besides ours [Christ Church], whereof the members were so perfectly satisfied with one another and so inoffensive to the other part of the University. All I have seen of the Fellows are both well natured and well bred; men admirably disposed as well to preserve peace and good neighbourhood among themselves, as to promote it wherever else they have any acquaintance" *(Letters,* 1:30). In such an atmosphere, Wesley could concentrate on further study and complete the degree of Master of Arts. On 14 February 1727, he delivered three lectures toward that purpose: *De Anima Brutorum* (on natural philosophy), *De Julio Caesare* (on moral philosophy), and *De Amore Dei* (on religion).

In preparing himself for the M.A., John Wesley demonstrated the degree to which the regimen of Susanna Wesley had become an essential part of his being and purpose. Almost immediately he developed a plan of study, one from which he determined never to depart. On Mondays and Tuesdays he read Greek and Latin, paying attention to the major writers of those languages; Wednesdays he set aside for logic and ethics, Thursdays and Fridays for Arabic and Hebrew, part of Fridays for metaphysics and natural philosophy, Saturdays to oratory and poetry, and Sundays to divinity.[9] During those sessions, he acquired the habit of setting down with care all passages he thought to be important. In that manner, he was able to achieve quick recall of such writers as Euclid; Dr. John Keill, Savilian Professor of Astronomy at Oxford; the Dutch geometrician and philosopher William James Gravesande, who taught the Newtonian system at Leyden; and, of course, Sir Isaac Newton himself. He was apparently so taken up with the latter two men of science and philosophy that he devoted some time to elementary experiments with optics; that may have been the beginning of his general interest in science that led him first to physic and medicine and then to electricity.

After earning the M.A. and returning to Lincoln College in late 1729, John Wesley settled in with his work as a tutor. The rector, Dr. John Morley, placed him in charge of eleven undergraduates; the degree to which he supervised their studies may be appreciated by a comment set forth in his journals over forty-five years later. Reacting, on 27 May 1776, to the brevity of the academic calendar then in effect at Scottish universities, November through May, Wesley lashed out, "So they *may* study five months in the year, and lounge all the rest. Oh where was the common sense of those who instituted such colleges? In the English colleges every one *may* reside all the year, as my pupils did; and I should have thought myself little better than a highwayman if I had not lectured them every day in the year but Sundays."[10] In addition to lessons, John Wesley was responsible, as junior Fellow, for presiding over (or moderating) the daily public disputations. Thus, he not only experienced the niceties of formal argument, but also learned to recognize various rhetorical devices, tricks, and fallacies. Considering all of the occasions between 1739 and 1791 when the Methodist leader would find himself called upon to defend his evangelical organization in the press and orally in public gatherings, he had reason to look back with a deep sense of appreciation upon his experiences in practical rhetoric at Lincoln College.

The last in the steady procession of Wesleys to enter Oxford arrived in 1726; as had his two brothers before him, Charles Wesley came to enter his name upon the rolls of Christ Church College. Unlike Samuel the younger and John, however, the eighteenth child and the last male of Susanna Wesley determined to take immediate and full advantage of the pleasures offered by both town and university. This does not mean that he sank to the depths of dissipation or depravity; most likely, at age nineteen and after more than nine years of close supervision at Westminster School and by his brother, the young scholar simply decided to drift along with the seekers of pleasure. Nevertheless, there exists no evidence that he abandoned, departed from, or even seriously deferred any of his scholarly interests and activities. "If I spoke to him about religion," reported John Wesley, "he would warmly answer, 'What, would you have me to be a saint all at once?' and would hear no more."[11] John's comment, combined with an increase in Charles's religious activities at Christ Church during 1728—meditation and weekly church attendance to receive the sacrament—has been traditionally employed by Wesleyan biographers and historians to emphasize the initial motives for the formation of the Oxford Holy Club. Nevertheless, Oxford Methodism did not come about solely because Charles Wesley needed a formal structure through which to transform himself from idler to serious minded and religious young man. His older brother may well have misinterpreted Charles's temporary laxness during the latter's first year and a half at Oxford, since, as we know, the souls of both Wesleys had been spoken for long before they left Epworth rectory.

From the outset, we need to realize that the credit for *organizing* the Holy Club belongs totally to Charles Wesley. The young scholar inaugurated its deliberations and projects sometime during May 1729, while John was still in Lincolnshire. After December 1729, when the older brother returned to Lincoln College and became one of its members, the leadership, direction, and responsibility for the actions of the group shifted from Charles to John. For Charles Wesley, in the spring of 1729, the Holy Club had served to accelerate the pace of his recently intensified religious interests. We may observe, with confidence, that prior to December 1729, the Holy Club was little more than a prayer group and a reading seminar; the regularity with which its members met, prayed, and studied earned them a variety of epithets: Sacramentarians, Oxonian Pietists,

Bible-bigots, Bible-moths, Godly Club, Holy Club, and, finally, Methodists. Interestingly enough, there exists the strong possibility that the term *methodist*, in the context of the Holy Club and its projects, may not have originated at Oxford in 1729. In a letter to John Wesley written sometime during 1784, Rev. Joseph Chapman—a Presbyterian minister at Staplehurst, Kent, who openly embraced Wesleyan Methodism—claimed that

The name "Methodist" is not a new name never before given to any religious people. Dr. [Edmund] Calamy, in one of his volumes of the *Ejected Ministers*, observes, "They called [ca. 1662] those who stood up for God Methodists." It is very remarkable that this was in the time of your own grandfather, John Wesley.[12]

In 1658, John Spencer, librarian of Sion College, London, published *Things New and Old; or, A Storehouse of Similies, Sentences, Allegories*, in which he asked, ". . . where are now our Anabaptists, and plain-pack-staff Methodists, who esteem all flowers of rhetoric in sermons, no better than stinking weeds?"[13] Actually, the term, in seventeenth-century popular English, referred to conservative physicians who followed established medical practice and methods, as opposed to those who favored new remedies. At any rate, Charles Wesley, for his part, identified the group simply as "Our Little Society," while John preferred the more distinct label of "Oxford Methodists."

No matter what the names associated with the Oxford Holy Club, none seemed able to bring about an increase in its membership or to promote its varied projects. Prior to John Wesley's return to Lincoln College in December 1729, Charles could count upon only two others, both of High Church persuasion, for regular attendance: William Morgan, commoner of Christ Church College, who left Oxford in 1731 and died on 26 August 1732, and whose memory received some degree of permanence in Samuel Wesley's poem on his death; and Robert Kirkham, of Merton College, a rather close friend of both Wesleys, who afterward drifted off to obscurity in a country curacy. Although the elder brother's reentrance into the scholarly existence of Oxford did not have an immediate effect upon the Holy Club, it would, in time, benefit from his association. Charles Wesley, recognizing his brother's position within the university, as well as his administrative abilities, quickly turned over the leadership of the group to him. John responded, by instituting at the outset, regular Sunday-evening meetings; he then moved to two evening sessions per week, and finally established gatherings every evening, from 6:00 until 9:00. The meetings themselves, obvious products of John Wesley's sense of discipline and organization, began with prayer; then followed a study of the Greek testament and of classical literature, a review of the previous day's work, and discussion of plans for the following day. On Sundays, the members focused upon matters of divinity; they fasted on Wednesdays and Fridays, received the Lord's Supper each week, and conducted thorough and regular self-examinations of their own conduct—both individually and as a group. [14]

By November 1730, membership in the Oxford Holy Club stood at five: the two Wesleys, Morgan, Kirkham, and an individual known (at least now) only as "Mr. Boyce," a member of a family residing in Oxfordshire. In August of that year, mainly through the efforts of young William Morgan, the club had expanded its activities to include charitable work, particularly regular visits to prisons and to hospitals. John Wesley, of course, always made certain to obtain prior approval from the parish minister before embarking on any such visits. From the beginning, he took extreme care not to run afoul of Establishment conventions.

A serious problem arose in August 1732. All members of the club but the Wesleys departed Oxford; the group appeared on the verge of extinction. However, the brothers continued to be visible in their pursuit of what Law had identified as the devout and holy life, with the result that almost immediately their ranks increased. [15] In 1732 alone, five men came forward: John Gambold, afterward to become a bishop in the Moravian church; Benjamin Ingham, who accompanied the Wesleys to Georgia and served as John's advisor; Thomas Broughton, later secretary to the Society for the Propagation of Christian Knowledge; John Clayton, a future vicar of Salford, one of John Wesley's first truly "religious" friends who assisted him with organizational and inspirational matters; and James Hervey of Lincoln College, who would engage Wesley and Wesleyan Methodism in literary controversy. In the next two years, four pupils of the Wesleys and John Clayton increased the size of the club, while in 1735, practically on the eve of the departure for Georgia, the most noteworthy addition came upon the scene in the person of twenty-one-year-old George Whitefield, then of Pembroke College. Interestingly, the future field-preacher of the Calvinist Meth-

odists entered the Holy Club by the same route as his future rivals—
William Law's *Serious Call to a Devout and Holy Life*. That volume
proved to have been one of the few items upon which, during the
next thirty-five years, Whitefield and the Wesleys could and would
agree.

Chapter Three
Autobiographical Writings

We need not read too far into the diaries, the journals, and the letters of John Wesley[1] before reaching the conclusion that within those volumes lies a considerable portion of the history of eighteenth-century British Methodism. In addition, we will discover that Wesley's attentiveness to the minutiae surrounding his daily thoughts and activities reveals insights into a wide variety of contexts not always associated with the founder and the leader of the Methodists. In other words, prejudgment and lack of knowledge have caused too many of us to assume that what held true for John Wesley was totally foreign to the majority of eighteenth-century British luminaries. We have been led to understand that Wesley stood outside the common denominators of theology, philosophy, literature, science, and the arts—that Pope, Johnson, Goldsmith, Horace Walpole, Priestley, Berkeley, Hume, Garrick, the brothers Adam, et al. lined up on one side of the social-theological-philosophical-intellectual arena, and John Wesley stood opposite, confronting his contemporaries with an evangelical sword of hell and damnation, dripping with the sweat of enthusiasm, spouting the rhetoric of the open fields of rural England! Such simply was not the case. Certainly, John Wesley had his arguments with his contemporaries; certainly he differed with their views and challenged their traditions. But he did not always differ or challenge. He had as much right to membership in the eighteenth century as did his peers—in certain instances, even more. And so we must learn to look at the autobiographical writings as justification not only for Wesley's thoughts and actions, but for his position within the overall scheme of eighteenth-century British social and intellectual history.

The practice of maintaining diaries and journals, as well as trying to make correspondence as literary as possible, was as much a part of eighteenth-century Europe as symmetrical gardens, snuff, gaming, masquerades, cheap gin, and stinking streets. No less a com-

mentator upon the British social and intellectual scene than Samuel
Johnson asserted that "a man loves to review his own mind. That
is the use of a diary, or journal." In support of such an observation,
James Boswell, as Johnson's occasional echo, responded, "And as a
lady adjusts her dress before a mirror, a man adjusts his character
by looking at his journal."[2] John Wesley surveyed the issue from
loftier, but seemingly more practical ground. In the preface to the
first published extract from his journals, he gives full credit to
Jeremy Taylor's *Holy Living* and *Holy Dying;* after reading those
tracts he writes, "I began to take a more exact account than I had
done before, of the manner wherein I spent my time, writing down
how I employed every hour."[3] Bishop Taylor, of course, did not
state outright that the pious man must keep a diary or journal;
rather, his concerns focused upon the maintenance of an exact account of how one spent his time. He advocated a review of one's
activities and thoughts by which that person might make amends
for his carelessness, renew his holy vows, and generally repair the
moral weak spots in his character.

The Diaries

Neither Bishop Taylor nor Johnson cared to set forth the dis-
tinctions between the terms *diary* and *journal;* for them (as well as
for us), the characteristics of one form as opposed to the other were
hardly noticeable or even necessary. For John Wesley, however, the
journal stood as a radical departure from the diary, even though he
intended the former to originate from, as well as to complement,
the latter. He began to keep a diary as early as April 1725, approximately four and a half months prior to his ordination as a
deacon in the Church of England. Aside from noting the important
events of the day, he inserted such items as lists of his pupils at
Lincoln College, timetables for various projects related to the Holy
Club, personal resolutions—even such information as a listing of
subscribers to his father's *Dissertationes* on Job.

The problem with Wesley's diaries, however, concerns not so
much the actual material set down on their pages, but the *manner*
in which Wesley presented that material. The entry for each day
reads as a fragment connected to its predecessors and successors only
by the obvious but fragile device of date. To compound the problem,
he did not write complete sentences (or anything resembling sen-

tences); instead, he relied upon a loose network of abbreviations, his own system of cipher (including Greek and Hebrew characters), and an antiquated shorthand system.[4] The last device came to him by way of the scholar and poet John Byrom, who developed his method while a student at Trinity College, Cambridge. Although Wesley had known of the shorthand technique created by James Weston in his 1727 *Stenography Completed* and even taught that form to his students at Lincoln College, he never adopted it for his own use. On Charles Wesley's suggestion, he adopted Byrom's method in 1736, during the time of his political problems with the magistrates of Savannah. As a result of the combinations of ciphers and systems, a diary entry is not always clear or meaningful, even when it has been completely "decoded." For example, on Friday, 7 August 1789, we note the following:

4.30   Prayed, tea; 5.30 chaise with Miss H, conversed; 7.30 chaise; 11 Hig gate, visited; 1 chaise; 1.45 at home, on business; 4.45 prayer, tea, conversed, prayer; 6 on business, prayed; 7 within; 8 supper, conversed; 9 prayer; 9.30.[5]

What emerges is a frame without substance. The decoding process provides us with the specifics of *when* and *where* he went; but Wesley, himself, has tantalized us by offering only vague notions of *what* he actually did when he got there!

If we allow ourselves to ramble too quickly through Wesley's diaries, we may be led to conclude that the writer became a slave to his own desire for order and method. It is essential, however, to realize immediately that Wesley composed the diaries for his own purposes. He simply did not wish to make public all of the details involving certain extremely personal matters, nor did he wish to reveal his indebtedness to close personal friends, particularly to a number of women whose identities he chose to conceal. Lest the scandalmongers of history become aroused unnecessarily, let it be known that in spite of the ciphers, allusions, and abbreviations found in the diaries—even the obscure references to *business*—Wesley had nothing to hide that would have reflected negatively upon his character. In enlisting a number of women into the ranks of Methodism, he naturally ran the risks of rumor and accusation; yet, for all of his "humanness," he had sufficient control—and sense—to avoid any indiscretion, potential or actual. The suggestions of misconduct or immorality that emerge from the fragments and ciphers of the diaries remain as suggestions; there is little of substance from which to develop an argument against the propriety of Wesley's conduct, although there were several attempts to do so during his lifetime. We must, therefore, be prepared to accept and to honor his motives for an elaborate scheme of concealment, even though certain items in the diaries flash vague and incomplete signals.

The exact areas of difference between Wesley's diaries and his journals may best be appreciated through simple comparison. One notices, for example, the following entries from each for Saturday, 18 October 1735, written on board the *Simmonds* only two days before it sailed out of Gravesend harbor for Savannah. First, the diary:

4½	Dressed; prayed; began Genesis 6; Deacon 3/4; writ to Varanese
7	Miss Sally Andrews, Sister Emilia 8; talked; writ to Salmon and
9	Clayton; 10. Falcon with Tackner; baptized him!
11	Delamotte Senior; read Whiston's Catechism.
1	½ dinner, 2½ on board. Conversed 3½. German. 4. Cabin.
4	Writ to Sister Kezia, Mr. Vernon, Mr. Hutcheson, my mother,
5	Rivington. 5½ talked. 6¼ devotion ½ sung 7. German with Tacknor.
7	Conversed, prayer, 9¼.

Now, notice the journal entry for the same date:

I baptized at his desire Ambrosius Tackner, aged thirty; he had received only lay baptism before. We dined on shore with Mr. Delamotte's father, who has come down on purpose to see him, and was now fully reconciled (which is of the power of God) to what he at first vigorously opposed.[6]

The *diary* entry for the eighteenth contains twenty-six activities (including rising, dressing, going to bed) and mentions fifteen persons; the *journal* entry records only two events. Of course, consultation with Wesley's letters will reveal the identities and contents of the vague diary entries and references, but that is not the point. For his journals, Wesley simply drew upon those details in the diary that he believed to be meaningful to a large number and variety of readers; those details upon which he expanded, both objectively and subjectively, he published for the enlightenment of all Methodists.

The remainder he held on to as fit only for his consumption. Because the journal entries bear a marked prose style, because they often appear as brief, self-contained essays, they deserve consideration as literary works, worthy of being ranked among the best representatives of that form.

The Journals

If his diaries allow John Wesley the luxury of intimacy, the journals provide him with the opportunity for exercising his skills as narrator, observer, and critical commentator. If the diaries force him to be cryptic, the journals permit him to bare to the world a prose style that indeed demonstrates his theological viewpoints and his total personality. He began the journals on Tuesday, 14 October 1735, one week before sailing for Georgia; the last journal entry is dated Sunday, 24 October 1790—fifty-five years, almost to the very day. Not surprisingly, the final note rings forth as an echo of the opening one: "Our end in leaving our native country," explained the thirty-two-year-old missionary, "was not to avoid want, God having given us plenty of temporal blessings, nor to gain riches nor honour, which we trust He will ever enable us to look on as no other than dung or dross; but singly this—to save our souls, to live wholly to the glory of God."[7] In his final entry (8:110), the eighty-seven-year-old patriarch of British Methodism records that he preached in Spitalfields church on the subject of Paul's epistle to the Ephesians (6:10–17): "Put on the whole armour of God . . . And Take the helmet of salvation, and the sword of the Spirit which is the word of God." Between the two declarations, Wesley applies his theological, political, historical, and literary values in a wide range of contexts, assuming the roles of judge and jury in the attempt to furnish practical examples for the general uplifting and enlightenment of those whom the nation knew, and often despised, as Methodists. An examination of three areas—books, historical personalities, and physical descriptions—will serve both to represent those contexts and to magnify Wesley's method of projecting his journals for public consumption.

The journals contain references to approximately 367 books, one-third of which are volumes classified as theology, religion, and church history. The remainder are concerned with such subjects as history, science, music, medicine, and travel. Essentially, Wesley assumes the role of grand critic or reviewer, his criteria for praise or censorship being his own emotional reaction and his judgment as to whether a writer or his work will contribute to the advancement of practical religion. Thus he reads James Boswell's *Journal of a Tour to the Island of Corsica* and exclaims, ". . . what a scene is opened therein! How little did we know of that brave people! How much less were we acquainted with the character of their general, Pascal Paoli; as great a lover of his country as Epaminondas,[8] and as great a general as Hannibal!" (5:292–93). Wesley reacts quickly to *legitimate* heroics, especially when he can filter the unfamiliar through classical analogies. However, he is a discriminating hero-worshiper. Sir Richard Blackmore's epic, *Prince Arthur*, "is not a contemptible poem, although by no means equal to his poem on the Creation, in which are many admirably fine strokes" (6:4–5). With the Boswell narrative and the Blackmore poem, he draws swift and general conclusions, offering little or no substantiation from the texts. Yet he does not always proceed in such a manner, especially if his reaction is negative. He can focus on a particular problem and dissect it with considerable attention to specifics. Thus he considers Dr. Henry Lee "both a learned and a sensible man," but his tract entitled *Sophron; or, Natural Characteristics of the Truth*

. . . will hardly come to a second impression, for these very obvious reasons: (1) his language is generally rough and unpleasing—frequently so obscure that one cannot pick out the meaning of a sentence without reading it twice or thrice over; (2) his periods are intolerably long, beyond all sense and reason—one period often containing ten or twenty, and sometime thirty, lines; (3) when he makes a pertinent remark he knows not when to have done with it, but spins it out without any pity to the reader; (4) many of his remarks, like those of his master, Mr. Hutchinson,[9] are utterly strained and unnatural, such as give pain to those who believe the Bible, and diversion to those who do not.   (6:5–6)

The journals are not simply storehouses of reaction to minor prose writers like Lee or second line poets like Richard Blackmore. John Wesley did, indeed, read works by major figures of his own times; in the majority of cases, however, the formalism of Charterhouse and Oxford, combined with the early rigidity of his mother's upbringing and his own developed sense of Puritanism, do not always allow him to appreciate fully the skills employed by men of advanced wit. He cannot, for example, see the irony behind Bernard Mandeville's *Fable of the Bees,* a piece that he believes exceeds even the goals of Niccolò Machiavelli. "The Italian," claims Wesley, "only recommends a few vices as useful to some particular men and on some particular occasions. But the Englishman loves and cordially recommends vice of every kind; not only as useful now and then, but as absolutely necessary at all times for all communities!" (4:157). He simply cannot understand either the meaning or the concept of sentimentalism or Laurence Sterne's last-gasp attempt to exhibit his own feelings. As "casually" as he peruses *A Sentimental Journey,* he denounces, "casually," the introduction of that new term, as well as the writer's entire effort: *"Sentimental!* what is that? It is not English; he might as well say *Continental.* It is not sense. It conveys no determinate idea; yet one fool makes many. And this nonsensical word (who would believe it?) is become a fashionable one! However, the book agrees full well with the title, for one is as queer as the other. For oddity, uncouthness, and unlikeliness to all the world beside, I suppose, the writer is without a rival" (5:445).

Throughout the journals, Wesley displays what can only be termed a fluctuation of critical temperaments. He will go so far as to judge writers not simply for what they actually produce, but for what he believes they represent. For instance, he not only despised everything about Voltaire the man—"certainly never was a more consummate coxcomb" (7:13)—he could not even endure the Frenchman's native tongue:

. . . by him I was more than ever convinced that the French is the poorest, meanest language in Europe; that it is more comparable to the German or Spanish than a bag-pipe is to an organ; and that, with regard to poetry in particular, considering the incorrigible uncouthness of their measure, and their always writing in rhyme (to say nothing of their vile double rhymes, nay, and frequent false rhymes), it is as impossible to write a fine poem in French as to make fine music upon a jews'-harp.   (4:188–89)

Still, Wesley is not so set in his critical ways, not so locked up in his own prejudices, that he will refuse to give a writer his due— or, more accurately, what Wesley *thought* to be his due, especially if the writer resided on the right side of the English Channel. Thus he admits to having "a very low opinion" of James Thomson's ability as a poet; "but looking into one of his tragedies, 'Edward and Eleanora,'[10] I was agreeably surprised. The sentiments are just and noble; the diction strong, smooth, and elegant; and the plot conducted with the utmost art, and wrought off in a most surprising manner. It is quite his masterpiece, and I really think might vie with any modern performance of the kind" (5:485). Had these last two sentences been written seven to nine years earlier, they would, in rhythm and language, have sounded like echoes of Samuel Johnson's *Lives of the Poets,*[11] although Wesley lacked Johnson's ability to create a feeling of fairness and almost total objectivity. Wesley's problem is that he chooses to recognize one of the more obscure of Thomson's works and to ignore the most noteworthy, *The Seasons.* We must remember, however, that the Methodist leader was not obliged to don the gown of literary critic or literary commentator. Instead, he followed his own criteria of virtue and morality, and in so doing made no distinction between a major and a minor poem or play.

In considering Wesley's journal commentary on writers and their works, we would be remiss if we did not turn for a moment to his use of quotations. A student both of classical rhetoric and the sermon address, he relied upon direct quotation to support, to illustrate, and to complement his observations, reactions, and opinions. Moreover, he produced the language and the thought of others seemingly without effort or forethought, for as one who read almost everything available and remembered a considerable portion of what he read, he did not have to spend time searching either his mind or his library. Thus, after reading William Law's *The Grounds and Reasons of Christian Regeneration,* he remarks, ". . . philosophical, speculative, precarious; Behmenish,[12] void, and vain! 'Oh what a fall is there!' " (2:297). At Epsom, after having dined with a friend at the latter's house, he reacts to the atmosphere of the place: "It is the most elegant spot I ever saw with my eyes, everything, within doors and without, being finished in the most exquisite taste. Surely nothing on earth can be more delightful; what will the possessor feel when he cries out: 'Must I then leave thee, Paradise? Then leave / These happy shades, and mansions fit for gods?' " (4:349). Into his journal for May 1757, he inserts an excerpt from a letter by Judith Beresford, one of his converts to Methodism who died at age twenty-four. "I believe," he states, "this was one of the last letters she wrote. Shortly after she was called hence.

> So unaffected, so composed a mind,
> So firm, yet soft, so strong yet so refined,
> Heaven, as its purest gold, with torture tried;
> The saint sustained it—but the woman died.[13] (4:210)

Of course, Wesley quoted from Scripture, and passages appear so frequently throughout his journals that examples are really unnecessary. The language of both Testaments became an integral part of his prose style, and in more than one instance he paraphrased or simply ignored the niceties of quotation marks. Although he did not take such liberties with other sources, he tended to misquote— not principally because he wished to alter a word or a phrase to suit his needs (which he actually did upon occasion), but because he commonly quoted from memory. For example, a stanza from a hymn by his brother Samuel, "On the Death of a Young Lady," reads,

> Let sickness blast and death devour,
> If heaven must recompense our pains:
> Perish the grass and fade the flower,
> Since firm the word of God remains.

Wesley, in his journal for 1 August 1776, changed the auxiliary verb *must* in the second line to *will* and the conjunctive adverb *Since* of the final line to *If* (5:179). Such seemingly minor alterations are sprinkled liberally upon the pages of his journals; whether or not most changes are intentional remains a matter of debate. What is not debatable, however, is that even minor changes did alter meaning.

In the journal comments upon historical figures, we may note what appears to be a peculiar quality of John Wesley's overall judgment of people, whether they be from the past or from his own present. Basically, he views the world's notables as though they were, or perhaps even ought to be, members of a Methodist society. In other words, he identifies the moral strengths and weaknesses of each, and then proceeds to praise or to condemn, as though he might have some influence upon the direction of the individual's body and soul. After reading about Frederick the Great in Voltaire's *Memoirs,* a work that would ignite his emotions with or without reference to historical personages, he cries out,

Surely so unnatural a brute never disgraced a throne before! "Cedite, Romani Catamiti! Cedite, Graii!"[14] A monster that made it a fixed rule to let no woman and no priest enter his palace; that not only gloried in the constant practice of sodomy himself, but made it free for all his subjects! What a pity his father had not beheaded him in his youth, and saved him from all this sin and shame! (7:13–14)

Obviously, Wesley would not be overwhelmed by one's rank, title, or office. His Puritan conscience penetrated what he believed to have been the superfutilities of human endeavor and the ornaments of human existence. After touring Walsingham Abbey in 1781, he could only conclude that "Had there been a grain of virtue or public spirit in Henry the Eighth, those noble buildings need not have been in ruin" (6:339). In general, his attitude toward persons of fame, power, and authority was contained, succinctly, in a passage from John Dyer's *Grongar Hill,* which he quoted in the journal:

> A little power,[15] a little sway,
> A sunbeam in a winter's day,
> Is all the great and mighty have
> Between the cradle and the grave. (4:402)

As one loyal to his church and to his nation, Wesley looked to the stability of the institution rather than toward the uncertainties of those who actually sat upon thrones. Thus he was not to be intimidated by the personalities of history.

Nevertheless, he could at times find reasons to embrace a hero or a heroine from history, a tendency that surprised even Wesley himself. In late April 1768, he came upon the historian William Tytler's vindication of Mary, Queen of Scots;[16] after that date, entries in the journals reveal the Methodist patriarch as an impassioned champion of Mary's innocence. At the outset, he simply summarized the evidence presented by Tytler (5:257); a week later, after having toured the royal palace at Scone, he noted "a bed and a set of hangings in the (once) royal apartment, which was wrought by poor Queen Mary while she was imprisoned in the castle of Lochleven. It is some of the finest needlework I ever saw, and plainly shows her exquisite skill and unwearied industry" (5:258). Over a year and a half later, he managed to elevate Mary from the level of purely moral "skill and unwearied industry" to that of sheer greatness; his point of view has shifted from admiration to adoration, from appreciation to love. Soon after reading William Guthrie's *History of Scotland,* he concluded that the "much-injured Queen appears to have been far the greatest woman of that age, exquisitely beautiful in her person, of a fine address, of a deep unaffected piety, and of a stronger understanding even in youth than Queen Elizabeth had at threescore" (5:348). A third historian, Gilbert Stuart—*History of Scotland from the Establishment of the Reformation till the Death of Queen Mary*—led him, in early 1786, to further proof that Mary "was not only one of the best Princesses then in Europe, but one of the most blameless, yea, and the most pious women!" (7:140). Six separate journal entries written over a span of eighteen years acclaim the virtues of a lady who had long since belonged to history; and that the writer of those opinions and observations was fast approaching the age when he, himself, would be beckoned by history raises an obvious question: Was Wesley trying to create an image from the past that would somehow fill his own romantic void, or was he really trying to hold on to the image of a woman of unquestionable piety whose own realm was limited to the four walls of a small rectory in Lincolnshire?

Perhaps the true strength of the journals is seen when Wesley functions as a recorder of the physical, when he writes description, or combines fact with reaction to fact. We may disagree with his points of view, but we can never challenge seriously his ability to grasp details, arrange them in an orderly manner, and infuse them with his natural tendency toward honesty and frankness. Here is a typical Wesley *exterior-interior* description:

The situation of the house[17] is very fine. It commands a large and beautiful prospect. Before the house is an open view; behind, a few acres of wood; but not laid out with any taste. The greenhouses are large, but I did not observe anything curious in them. The front of the house is large and magnificent, but not yet finished. The entrance is noble, the saloon exceeding grand, and so are several of the apartments. Few of the pictures are striking. I think none of them to be compared with some in Fonmon Castle. The most extraordinary thing I saw was the stables; a square fit for a royal palace, all built of fine stone, and near as large as the old Quadrangle at Christ Church in Oxford. But for what use were these built? To show that the owner had near three-score thousand pounds a year! Oh, how much treasure might he have laid up in heaven, with all this mammon of unrighteousness! (7:183–85)

We realize rather quickly that even in such an informal prose form as a journal entry, Wesley has carefully manipulated almost every example toward a moralistic finale. For his purposes—public education and enlightenment—the line between a journal intended for publication and an address delivered from a pulpit was indeed indistinct.

Even the very shrines of England cannot escape Wesley's ultra-critical eye. In February 1764, he "took a serious walk through the tombs in Westminster Abbey. What heaps of unmeaning stone and marble!" (5:46). Another occasion found him strolling through the British Museum, where "One large room is filled from top to bottom with things brought from Otaheite; two or three more with things dug out of the ruins of Herculaneum! Seven huge apartments are filled with curious books, five with manuscripts, two with fossils of all sorts, and the rest with various animals. But what account will a man give to the Judge of quick and dead for a life spent in collecting all these?" (6:301). A not so sacred, but yet popular shrine, Cox's Museum, stood in Spring Garden, London, and was known for its unique timepieces and jeweled ornaments. Wesley brushed aside the place with the same contempt: "I cannot say my expectation was disappointed; for I expected nothing, and I found nothing but a heap of pretty, glittering trifles, prepared at an immense expense. For what end? To please the fancy of fine ladies and pretty gentlemen" (5:499).

If so much of John Wesley's journal may appear to be negative—attacks upon bad books, unreasonable writers, immoral personages, wasteful institutions—there may be some truth to the accusation prevalent during the 1920s and 1930s that the founder and leader of Methodism lacked a sense of humor. Essentially that is true, but a lack of humor does not necessarily engender negative opinions and observations. Wesley's problem was that following his undergraduate years at Christ Church, he plunged into a course of life dominated and controlled by absolute seriousness. Pope, Swift, Gay, Johnson, Goldsmith, Sheridan—any of a hundred of his contemporaries—would have laughed at the likes of Henry Lee, literary French, Thomson's plays, Frederick the Great, or Cox's Museum; or, seen another way, their contempt and bitterness would have been masked by laughter. Unfortunately, Wesley found no release through the subtleties of satire or the explosiveness of laughter; he had neither the wit nor the stomach for ridicule or burlesque. His sole weapon was the rapier of what can only be termed *moral prose,* whether essay, letter, or journal entry. His target was the moral conscience of a nation.

Further, Wesley, living in a century wherein men and women had and spent more time for diversion than for practical employment, stood almost alone as a man of little leisure. Rarely did he find a moment for laughter, play, or love. Caught up in what he believed to be the noblest of all purposes—to serve God—he could discover no room, even among the pages of his journals, for intellectual relaxation. Thus he crammed those journals with facts and reactions to facts, identifying for his readers what they should emulate and what they should ignore. Whether in a 250-word journal entry or in a full-length, formal prose tract, Wesley had no room for what he considered mere fads and fashions.

The Letters

As both the organizational and the intellectual leader of the British Methodists, John Wesley viewed the writing of letters as the essential means for achieving simple and practical ends. He dispatched letters *crescendo, fortissimo, con molto espressione*—at least 2,700 of them between 3 November 1721 and 24 February 1791. He wrote to almost everyone, from his mother to the King of England; he sent letters in almost every direction, to Basingstoke and the Isle of Wight, to Savannah and Boston. At one extreme he rushed off abrupt directives, as though a general were crisply issuing orders to his troops in the field: "Dear Simon,—You shall be in Oxfordshire. Adieu."[18] At the other extreme is his 1749 letter to Conyers Middleton, a tract of approximately 38,500 words in opposition to Middleton's *A Free Inquiry into the Miraculous Powers* of 1748; Wesley postponed a voyage to Rotterdam and spent the twenty days from 4 to 24 January 1749 at work on the epistle (2:312–88). Between the single-sentence directive and the fully developed essay stands the bulk of Wesley's correspondence: the leader of a significant religious movement communicating with his subordinates scattered about the island-kingdom, the self-appointed guardian of his nation's morals actively engaged in pointing Britons of both sexes and of all persuasions in the direction of heaven.

Wesley's letters, even more than his journals, reflect the character of their writer: concise, accurate, forcible, and clear. Thus, the most obvious quality of his epistolary style, sheer simplicity, demonstrates

that he never gave stature to the modes of circumvention or orna-
mentation. In other words, he attacked all problems immediately,
refusing to waste precious time (his own or the reader's) with in-
troductory amenities and trifles. Writing to his brother Charles
from London on 26 December 1761, he begins, "Dear Brother,—
Spend as many hours in the congregation as you will or can. But
exercise alone will strengthen *your lungs*. Or electrifying, which I
wonder you did not try long ago. Never start at its being a quack
medicine. I desire no other, particularly since I was so nearly mur-
dered of being cured of my ague *secundum artem*. You should always
(and I hope you do) write standing and sloping" (4:166). The tone
belongs to an individual who spent in excess of fifty years traveling,
preaching, administering, writing, determined to account for each
minute of his eighteen- or nineteen-hour day, and equally determined to safeguard his spiritual and physical well-being and to see
that his followers did the same.

The tone of the letters does not always remain consistent, however,
especially when the relationship between writer and recipient is
extremely personal, complex, or even sensitive. For example, Wesley
could control his male preachers, stewards, and trustees; if they
failed to respond to his directives or to conduct themselves according
to his strict standards, he simply removed them. On the other hand,
he could not always settle, with equal expedition, problems that
arose with certain women; with them, he could not always act as
organizational administrator or spiritual leader. In letters to Susanna
Wesley, we observe the dutiful son laying his problems and his fears
before the sacred altar of motherhood; to Sophia Christiana Hopkey,
whom he wanted to marry, and to Mrs. Molly Vazielle, whom he
did marry, he poured forth the frustrations resulting from the rejection of early love and the failure of marriage. In his dealings with
the women close to him, Wesley appeared, at least on paper, un-
comfortable; they fired his passion, but, more often, drove him to
despair. Naturally, his letters to those women reflect, sometimes
even generate, that discomfort, passion, and despair.

Between 23 September 1723 and 6 July 1738, Wesley wrote at
least twenty letters to his mother, most of which originated from
Oxford and were composed prior to his evangelical conversion and
the development of Methodism. Thus, Susanna Wesley became a
natural sounding-board for her son's spiritual inquiries and dilem-
mas. At the outset, the letters appear insignificant, focusing upon

such matters as the smallpox at Oxford, nosebleeds, the price of fruit, street robbers, Jack Shepherd's escape from Newgate, the weather, needlessly lengthy anecdotes, brief book reviews, attempts to define faith and predestination. Then, by early 1732, the subjects begin to strike a more urgent tone, as Wesley came to grips with a problem that eventually manifests itself as the essence of British Methodism: the rerouting of his attention from the contemporary social situation to a clear focus upon a better state, one in which the individual receives the benefits of Christ's incarnation and passion: "But how?" he asks his mother in February 1732. "What is the surest and the shortest way? Is it not to be humble? Surely this is a large step in the way. But the question recurs, How am I to do this? To own the necessity of it is not to be humble. In many things you have interceded for me and prevailed. Who knows but in this too you may be successful? If you can spare me only that little part of Thursday evening which you formerly bestowed upon me in another manner, I doubt not but it would be as useful now for correcting my heart as it was then for forming my judgment" (1:119–20). Recalling those childhood days at Epworth rectory, twenty years ago, when Susanna Wesley set apart some time every evening to converse and to counsel with one of her children (John's turn coming on Thursdays), the twenty-eight-year-old son—now fully ordained as a priest of the Church and the holder of an advanced degree in philosophy and religion—asks once again to come to his mother's bosom.

The two years prior to the voyage for Georgia (October 1735) proved difficult for Wesley; he was not certain how long he could hold on to those of his students at Lincoln College who had become active in the Holy Club, and his father began to press him to take on the duties as rector of Epworth and Wroote. Decisions had to be made, both practical and spiritual. "At this season especially," wrote Wesley to his mother on 15 February 1733, "I would not neglect any help for mortifying the flesh and the lusts thereof, for throwing off the affections of the earthly Adam, and putting on the image of the heavenly. If I am to be surrounded with the snares of flesh and blood, yet many years, will you not give me the best advices to break through them that you can?" (1:134). Almost a year later, on 13 January 1735, he again sought Susanna Wesley's heart, this time on a matter relating to Christian liberty; he "had a great deal of conversation lately on the subject . . . and should be glad of your thoughts as to the several notions of it which good men entertain" (1:178). Interestingly, after Wesley had determined to leave Lincoln College and to sail with James Oglethorpe to Georgia—and, after returning from America to visit with Count Zinzendorf and his Moravians in German—the remaining correspondence with his mother no longer stresses the need for intellectual advice or for spiritual assistance. Instead, letters from Savannah, Amsterdam, Cologne, and Utph seem almost purely topographical and descriptive. For the moment, at least, Wesley could convey to his mother the impression of moving toward a purpose in life and away from the anxiety of his last years at Oxford.

Yet, Wesley's exercises in soul-searching near the junction of the Cherwell and the Thames seem trifles when set beside the problems he encountered during his twenty-two months in the Georgia colony. We may pass over two difficulties—the failure to achieve any headway in his attempts to convert the Indians, and the collision with the trustees of the colony that led to his return to England—to settle upon a third, the unfortunate relationship with Sophia Christiana Hopkey. Wesley, then but three months short of his thirty-third birthday, met Miss Hopkey, only slightly over eighteen, at Savannah on 13 March 1736, five weeks or so after his arrival in Georgia. The majority of sources agree upon her charm and piety, as well as the origins of her agitated state at the time of the meeting: first, residence with her aunt and uncle—the latter, Thomas Causton, the unpopular chief magistrate of the colony; second, an abortive love affair with one Thomas Mellichamp, her uncle's clerk, who threatened violence upon the girl should she involve herself with another man. [19] The Caustons determined to place their niece in the charge of the young minister and Oxford don, who would function as her tutor and spiritual counselor. Thus she came daily to his house, where he taught her French, identified the proper highways to eternal salvation, read to her from William Law's *Christian Perfection,* and, within a year, reached the point of asking for her hand in marriage. However, his friends at Savannah, who were also Causton's political opponents, as well as self-appointed guardians of Wesley's celibacy, argued against the proposed union. On 4 February 1737, Benjamin Ingham sent him to Irene, four miles from Savannah, to ponder his future. There, Wesley concluded that he could not marry anyone until he had at least begun his missionary work among the Indians. The delay proved fatal; on 12 March 1737,

Sophia, caught between Mellichamp's threats and Wesley's idealism, wed William Williamson. The rejected missionary, trying to convince himself that he had somehow been saved from an unsuitable marriage, sought consolation in his prayers, his garden, and Bishop Joseph Hall's *Meditation on Heaven.*

The actual trauma of the relationship reveals itself in one section of Wesley's journals (1:181–337), but three letters to Sophia Hopkey establish the degree to which the matter vexed him. With Susanna Wesley, his spiritual advisor, an ocean distant, he was forced to rely upon the only other guidance available. "I find, Miss Sophy," wrote Wesley from Irene, "I can't take fire into my bosom and not be burnt. I am therefore retiring for a while to desire the direction of God. Join with me, my friend, in fervent prayer that He would show me what is best to be done" (1:211). Had one or the other left Savannah after Sophia's marriage, the affair undoubtedly would have ended without further comment. The Williamsons remained, however, which meant that Sophia continued as one of Wesley's parishioners. He may have lost her heart, but he still had jurisdiction over her soul.

Observing some deterioration in the young lady's religious habits, Wesley, in the summer of 1737, repelled her from the Holy Communion. Writing to Sophia on 5 July, he appears to be wearing the mantle of the cleric, while continuing to endure the pains of the rejected suitor. On the one hand, he dislikes "(1) your neglect of half the public service . . . (2) your neglect of fasting . . . (3) your neglect of almost half the opportunity of communicating . . ." (1:224). On the other,

. . . (1) You told me over and over you had entirely conquered your inclination for Mr. Mellichamp. Yet at that very time you had not conquered it. (2) You told me frequently you had no design to marry Mr. Williamson. Yet at the very time you spoke you had the design. (3) In order to conceal both these things from me, you went through a course of deliberate dissimulation. Oh how fallen! How changed! Surely there was a time in Miss Sophy's life when there was no guile. (1:224–25)

The letter represents John Wesley's method for handling complex and delicate issues: simply, he elevated himself above the problem, filtered it through his sense of moral righteousness, directed in clear prose the blame or the solution toward what he believed to be the proper mark, and then removed the matter from his area of concern, either permanently or for the moment. Certainly, Sophia Christiana Hopkey would leave a scar upon his heart, but by that time he had developed a sense of higher responsibility that would provide the proper balm. "And when you have openly declared yourself to have truly repented," he wrote on 11 August 1737, "I will administer to you the mysteries of God" (1:226). Having taken a tight hold upon his *official* designation as the agent of the Church of England for Savannah, Wesley could than place into the files of history his first extended encounter with love.

If the leader of the British Methodists gained little satisfaction from the Sophia Hopkey Williamson affair, his marriage, fourteen years later, would yield him even less. On 18 February 1751, John Wesley married Mrs. Molly Vazielle, widow of a London merchant, mother of four children, and a woman with nothing to recommend her in terms of appearance, education, or intelligence. Ambrose Vazielle had left her a house in Threadneedle Street, London, and £10,000, but the sum turned out to be secured to the children; thus, none of the money found its way into Wesley's own accounts or into the coffers of the Methodist societies.[20] Most probably, Wesley, then age forty-eight, was attracted by her widow's garb, the familiar attire worn by his mother during the last seven years of her life; he dreaded high-born ladies and adorned belles, preferring to fix his gaze upon passive and drab women, particularly widows. The first and last Mrs. John Wesley certainly may have been drab, but she proved hardly passive. At the outset of their union, she accompanied her husband on his travels, but she could (or would) not adapt to fluctuating weather, primitive travel conditions, and anti-Methodist demonstrations. In addition, finding other women engaged in Methodist activities, she immediately misinterpreted her husband's intentions toward female lay preachers and teachers; such jealousy transformed her into an absolute shrew, and in January 1758 the two parted company. After brief periods of reconciliation—totally different from those Wesley may have remembered between Samuel and Susanna Wesley, and with totally different results—and after recurrences of the same jealousies, Molly Wesley departed in 1771 for the final time. On Friday, 12 October 1781, Wesley noted, almost casually, "I came to London and was informed that my wife died on Monday [8 October]. This evening she was buried, though I was not informed of it till a day or two after."[21]

Twenty-two extant letters from Wesley to his wife serve as the principal instruments for tracing the deterioration of a marriage that, although it endured technically for thirty years, should never have occurred at all. The first eight letters, written between 27 March 1751 and 24 April 1757, convey the image of an harmonious existence, albeit one in which Wesley spent time trying to convince Molly that he did indeed love and trust her. "Have not *you* above all people in the world," he asked in his initial epistle, "a right to hear from me as soon as possibly I can? You have surely a right to every proof of love I can give and to all the little help which is in my power. For you have given me even your own self " (3:63). A year later, the relationship shows signs of having been strengthened, principally because the two had been traveling together in and around Newcastle-upon-Tyne. In mid-May 1752, Molly went alone to Bristol, called there as a result of her son's illness; Wesley's letter to her a week later on 22 May reflects what was for him an almost euphoric state, tempered somewhat by the usual security stationed around his sense of self-responsibility:

My dear Love,—Give the glory to God. Your name is precious among this people. They talk of you much, and know not how to commend you enough. . . . Their way of mentioning you often brings tears into my eyes. Bless God for all His benefits. I rejoice for your sake; but I condemn myself. I have not made such use of the time we have been together as I might have done. The thing which I feared has come upon me. I have not conversed with you so seriously as I ought. I ought always to speak seriously and weightily with you, as I would with my guardian angel. Undoubtedly it is the will of God that we should be as guardian angels to each other. O what a union is that whereby we are united! The resemblance even between that of Christ and His Church. And can I laugh or trifle a moment when with you? O let that moment return no more!

(3:91–92)

How difficult it must have been for Molly Vazielle, despite her own shortcomings; in marrying John Wesley, she had joined herself to one already wed to the spirit and to the work of God. Despite his kind words and references to mutual guardian angelship, he functioned on a level far above her domestic and mundane values. She simply could not compete!

After Molly's initial departure in January 1758, Wesley's letters to her assume the quality of rhetorical exercises, lessons from the apostle to his disobedient subordinate. From Coleford, on 23 October 1759, "I will tell you simply and plainly the things which I dislike. If you remove them, well. If not, I am but where I was" (4:75). Even in the midst of serious domestic upheaval, Wesley holds firm to rhetorical method. He proceeds to list ten grievances, ranging from Molly's public disclosure of his personal correspondence to her display of bitterness toward his friends; those are followed by an equal number of remedies—"advice which I now give you in the fear of God and in tender love to your soul" (4:78). On 23 March 1760, he reprimands his wife for failing to perform the duties required of their marriage, concluding that "every act of disobedience is an act of rebellion against God and the King, as well as against Your affectionate Husband" (4:89). The struggle continued for another fourteen years; Wesley held to a firm course, a willingness for patience in order to save something from this grand mistake, even though the salvage operation had to be conducted only upon his own terms. "Be content to be a private, insignificant person, known and loved by God and me. Attempt no more to abridge me of the liberty which I claim by the laws of God and man. Leave *me* to be governed by God and my own conscience. Then shall I govern *you* with gentle sway, and show that I do indeed love you, even as Christ the Church" (6:102).

However, even John Wesley could exhaust his storehouse of patience; by the autumn of 1778, he had had enough of Ambrose Vazielle's widow. On 2 October 1778, from Bristol, he addressed her for the final time, strong reproof for having again published certain of his private papers; the letter lacks both opening and closing salutation: "If you were to live a thousand years twice told, you could not undo the mischief which you have done. And till you have done all you can towards it, I bid you Farewell!" (6:322; 8:274). At age seventy-five, Wesley had come to realize fully the price that had been extracted from him by British Methodism: man's most basic pleasure and the results thereof, love and marriage, were never to be his.

The journals and letters of John Wesley reveal that their author had learned, early in his career, how essential they were to expediting his evangelical mission. He directed the style and the content to specific needs of a large and diverse group of followers, a proportion of whom were not always faithful to their cause. In adapting the theses of individual letters and journal entries to current times and to current places, he nonetheless focused upon universal themes. Thus he viewed both journals and letters (and at times even the diaries) as complements to institutional organization. Yet, as we have seen, Wesley's autobiographical writings (to use Pope's terms) conveyed the *sound* as well as the sense. He worked hard to forge a balance of tenderness, passion, and persuasion on the one hand and the devices of classical rhetoric (question, antithesis, example) on the other.

In addition to the obvious tendencies toward Puritan rigidity and prejudgment, Wesley possessed and expressed a sense of frankness and directness. Both the journals and the letters reflect the spirit of a man not afraid of humility or honest criticism and willing to receive advice, as well as to give it. "Having at length a few hours to spare," he wrote to Rev. Henry Venn on 22 July 1763, "I sit down to answer your last, which was particularly acceptable to me, because it was wrote with so great openness. I shall write with the same. And herein you and I are just fit to converse together, because we both like to speak blunt and plain, without going a great way round about. . . . I want you to understand me inside and out. Then I say, *Sic sum: si placeo, utere.*"[22] Such sentiments underscore the advantage of reading the journals and letters of John Wesley: because he wrote plainly of what he knew and of what he observed, the drama of the Evangelical Revival in eighteenth-century England, Ireland, and Wales unfolds before us, a procession of players led by the diminutive Fellow of Lincoln College, accompanied by the rhythmic vibrations from the mind and heart of his younger brother, and composed of tens of thousands of refugees from the outmoded institutions of the Establishment. Thus Wesley's journals and letters constitute an essential part of the historical literature of the period, while at the same time they provide the necessary ingredients for perpetuating the image of a great man.

Chapter Four
Hymns and Occasional Verse

At some point between 1737 and 1739—between the publication of John Wesley's *A Collection of Psalms and Hymns* and John and Charles Wesley's *Hymns and Sacred Poems*[1]—the two brothers entered into an agreement whereby their poetry would be published under both their names. The purpose of such an agreement seems to have been to avoid any discussion or argument, both within and without the boundaries of Methodism, about the literary reputation of one or the other. Certainly, we admire such self-effacement in an age when the *literati* vied with one another for patronage and recognition by a relatively small reading public. However, the Wesleys' pact not to specify authorship (which they consented to break on two occasions) has produced a series of interesting but not always profitable exercises for bibliographers, textual scholars, and critical commentators.

Painstaking reviews of diaries, journals, and letters, along with some attempts to identify the stylistic similarities between John and Charles Wesley, have not yielded substantive results. For example, Henry Bett, a thorough and respected scholar of Methodist poetry, believed that he was "able, through a patient examination of hymns that are known to be John Wesley's, to establish canons that may serve to identify some other of the hymns as his, while generally confirming the belief that the bulk of the hymns are the work of Charles." Ever so carefully, Bett plods through the labyrinths of measure, end rhymes, syllabic division, sentence lengths, compounds, numbers of syllables, prefixes, triads, phrasings, and constructions. While plodding, he sometimes stumbles over his own feet. At one point, after listing a dozen hymns that ought, according to his canons, to belong to *John* Wesley, he concludes, "Anything like detailed proof is naturally impossible here."[2] Exactly! Given the lack of definite evidence that will challenge (and/or refute) what is already known, we can therefore proceed to examine the poetry of the Wesleys on the basis of that evidence known to have existed for almost two hundred years.

Generally, Charles Wesley deserves the title of "The Bard of Methodism." John Wesley, although he did produce some original verse, principally concerned himself with editing collections of hymns and poems, translating hymns and poems from both classical and modern sources, and revising certain of his brother's poetical pieces. The total output of the two is probably in excess of 8,900 separate poems; the majority came from the pen of Charles, and approximately five hundred of those continue to be found in a large and representative number of hymn collections for public worship. Obviously, not all of the poems merit explication, analysis, or even mention, a fact that helps us determine upon which brother to concentrate when discussing the entire matter of Wesleyan poetry.

The extant hymns aand poems[3] of Charles Wesley echo the essence of the Evangelical Revival of eighteenth-century Britain. Certainly, not every one of the poems evinces the same degree of quality, but together—especially when viewed in the light of congregational hymnody—the entire canon conveys the intensity of the poet's deep personal feelings. Few subjects or occasions escaped his notice: his own religious conversion and marriage; domestic upheavals from panics, earthquakes, religious riots, rumored foreign invasion; festivals of the Church of England and doctrines of the faith; scenes from and paraphrases of Scriptures; deaths of friends; the education of children; the effects of local surroundings. Charles Wesley could adapt those subjects, experiences, and occasions to congregational worship because he easily maneuvered the instruments necessary to shape the English hymn: simple diction, lucid construction, resonant lines, emphasis upon repetition of plain Gospel truth, and poetic images that could be understood by a large number of people representing *all* ranks and levels of eighteenth-century British society. As was true of his elder brother John, Charles Wesley spent little time contemplating and transmitting abstract themes. Instead, he robed himself in the linguistic habits of the personal and the concrete. Thus his poetry reflected the experiences of thousands of believers and an equal number of others who struggled to believe.

Because the poetry of Charles Wesley sounds the notes of the Evangelical Revival, we need to observe it within the total context of that movement. In other words, we need to consider contemporary events as well as theological ideals, the social as well as the religious background against which Wesley wrote. Eighteenth-century British Methodism was characterized by the devoutness of its leaders and their immediate subordinates, their compassion and their collective belief in the propriety of church reform. But eighteenth-century Methodism was also characterized by its heavy reliance upon the details and the language of Scriptures—of both the Old and the New Testaments; for the poetry of Charles Wesley forced Britons to transcend ecclesiastical divisions and theological controversies. Thus the poet of Methodism transmitted the language and developed the imagery of the patriarchs, of the prophets, of the Gospels, of the epistles. Hebrew and early Christian societies came alive in the poetry of Charles Wesley, and biblical events pointed out important parallels with the major occurrences of the poet's own time. In one sense, the poetry of Charles Wesley, the poetry of Methodism, was the call for a new day:

> Britons, arise with one accord,
> And learn the glory of the Lord!
> The Lord, from whom salvation came,
> Doth justly all your praises claim:
> With humble heart and thankful voice
> Rejoice aright, to God rejoice.[4]

Occasional Verse

"Everything has its day," wrote Samuel Johnson in his *Life of Prior*. "Through the reigns of William and Anne no prosperous event passed undignified by poetry."[5] Johnson had in mind such events as the death of Queen Mary in 1695, mourned in verse by at least fifteen poets (including Samuel Wesley the elder), and the War of the Spanish Succession (1701–1713), with its hero, John Churchill, Duke of Marlborough, and his succession of victories in Bavaria and Flanders: Blenheim, Ramillies, Oudenarde, and Malplaquet. England's efforts against France, Spain, and Bavaria to determine a monarch for Spain provided considerable fuel for the poetic kilns of at least fifty versifiers, as Whigs and Tories explored every means possible for achieving some degree of credit for Marlborough's triumphs. Not surprisingly, the cascade of poetic tears for Mary evaporated quickly, while the forced metaphors in support of British arms in Bavaria and Flanders passed, as quickly, into obscurity. As any schoolboy should know, persons possessed of little capacity for poetry, even though their hearts and their minds seek the heights of honest expression, have difficulty rising to the significance of a contemporary political or military event. That proves especially true when the details of the occasion, though important, appear totally unfamiliar to the poet, or when the poet obscures those events in total unfamiliarity.

From about mid-century onward, the versifiers of Britain tended toward "higher" subjects upon which to construct their themes, leaving the exploits of cabinet ministers and soldiers to the imaginations of the prose writers. Thus Charles Wesley devoted considerable time and effort to preserve not only the meaning of doctrinal struggles surrounding Methodism in eighteenth-century Britain, but also to capture familiar human reactions to natural phenomena and national problems existing between 1744 and 1788. Unlike those earlier poets of Anne who strived to dignify their own reputations, Wesley was beholden to no government minister or political faction; his hymns and poems on all subjects reflected an authentic desire to record the beliefs of his own mind and the feelings of his own heart. Certainly, he held the laurel as the chief poet of Methodism, and he clearly complemented the work of his older brother; yet, as did his brother, Charles Wesley remained loyal to his nation, sovereign, and Church. His emotions, not his ambitions, found their best outlet in his poetry. Earthquakes, panics, domestic riots, rumors of foreign invasion, the triumphs and even the defeats of British arms: all came within Charles Wesley's view and furnished, at least for him, legitimate occasions for the sincere exercise of his poetic talents.

One of the earliest of such occasions presented itself in March 1744, when 15,000 French headed by Maurice, Comte de Saxe, and Prince Charles Edward, the twenty-four-year-old Young Pretender, sailed from Dunkirk for Scotland. The ships, however, were driven back by storms. In July 1745, against the advice of the French, the Pretender landed in Scotland, accompanied by only seven attendants, and raised his standard at Glenfinnan. The government, caught unprepared, could muster only 1,500 men against the Jacobites; the prince quickly captured Edinburgh and on 21 September defeated Sir John Cope at Prestonpans. By then, Charles Edward had raised 5,500 supporters, whom he directed toward England; December found him as far south as Derby. Although news reports led to panic among the citizens of London, there was

little justification for worry, since only about 300 Britons had rallied
to the Jacobite cause, and the prince's Scottish followers were de-
serting him in quick order. By December, the Pretender was back
in Sterling, and in April the young Duke of Cumberland defeated
him at Culloden.

Charles Wesley's *Hymns for Times of Trouble and Persecution,* published first in 1744 and reissued in 1745, served as the poet's reaction
to the threatened invasion by the French fleet. Of the thirteen hymns
in this small collection, three bear the heading "A Prayer for His
Majesty King George"; a fourth, and the final hymn of the volume,
is entitled "For the King and His Royal Family." The closing stanza
of the last piece (lines 31–36) establishes clearly Wesley's fundamental view toward his nation and his sovereign:

> Secure us of his royal race
> A man to stand before Thy face,
> And exercise Thy power;
> With wealth, prosperity and peace,
> Our nation and our church to bless,
> Till time shall be no more.
> (*PW,* 4:26)

Here, the poet's loyalty to Britain, George II, and the Church of
England rings forth on the notes of simple but direct language,
while the tone remains steady and confident. He appeals directly
to God as protector and preserver of kings and nations. Yet, in the
face of threatened Popish invasion, the tone is obviously militant;
the poet rises in defiance, casting aside the general mood of doubt
and fear:

> Defeat, confound, oppress
> The troubles of his peace;
> Blast their every vain design;
> 'Stablish Thou his quiet throne;
> Tell his foes—"This soul is Mine,
> Touch not Mine annointed one."
> (*PW,* 4:23)

The lines come forth almost as a sermon in rhyme, directed to an
audience of common men and women who need to recognize the
"Fountain of power, from whom descends / The regal dignity di-

vine!" (*PW*, 4:23). Thus the language of the hymnodist, as familiar to its readers and singers as the words from the Bible, seeks to rally a nation almost paralyzed with fear from rumors of invasion.

Wesley wrote seven poems following the Battle of Culloden, all published as *Hymns for the Public Thanksgiving-Day, October 9, 1746.* Essentially the tone of the volume is one of exuberance:

> Britons, rejoice, the Lord is King!
> The Lord of Hosts and nations sing,
> Whose arm hath now your foes o'erthrown;
> > (*PW*, 4:93)

But the poet quickly directs his readers to the realization that Culloden represented not simply the triumph of one human force over another; rather,

> Ascribe the praise to God alone,
> The Giver of success proclaim,
> And shout your thanks in Jesus' name!
> > (*PW*, 4:93)

The vision of the soldier-conqueror as "Our godlike leader," which Joseph Addison had borrowed from Homer and thrust into his *Campaign* (1704) to describe Marlborough, gives way to Charles Wesley's concept of the Christian knight (the Duke of Cumberland) who derives his courage *from* God:

> O let him thankfully submit
> To lay his laurels at Thy feet,
> By faith a Christian hero stand,
> And hang on Thine all-ruling hand,
> Supporter of his father's throne,
> Upheld himself by Thee alone!
> > (*PW*, 4:98)

More than a Christian hero, William exists as a defender of Protestantism, although the slaughter of 2,000 Highlanders in less than one-half hour, plus the relentless pursuit and extinction of survivors and other rebels, served to tarnish his image as a "Christian hero." Nonetheless, Wesley holds to the view of the 1745 uprising as a project undertaken by traitors and Papists, supported by *"Spanish* gold, and *Gallic* pride, / And *Holy Church* is on their side" (*PW,* 4:97). Through the intervention of a Protestant God, "Lo! the audacious hopes of *Rome* / Rush headlong to their instant doom" (*PW,* 4:97), much like Milton's Satan being hurled out of Heaven after his vain attempt to challenge God. Again the Methodist poet clings to clear and direct language, reenforced only by the obvious imagery of the Bible. With God always in his sight, he easily reduces the generalizations of historical events to quick and decisive Divine acts. Little remains for inquiry or debate; the "lightning from His eye" (*PW,* 4:97), the only legitimate force, is absolute.

Fifteen years later, in the autumn of 1759, England once more faced the prospect of invasion. On 14 November, Admiral Hubert de Brienne, Comte de Conflans, headed the main French fleet of twenty-two vessels out of Brest harbor in an attempt to release his transports at Rochefort and then push on for England. He was pursued by Admiral Edward Hawke, in command of twenty-three ships of the Channel Fleet, and overtaken at Quiberon Bay, in Brittany. On 20 November, six of Conflans's ships were either taken, sunk, or wrecked; the remainder fled. The British victory resulted in the termination of the French fleet as an effective offensive force for the remainder of the Seven Years' War. The engagement prompted two series of poems from Charles Wesley: *Hymns on the Expected Invasion* (1759) and *Hymns To Be Used on the Thanksgiving-Day, November 29, and After It* (1759).

Both content and language of the 1759 volumes are similar to the pieces on the Jacobite uprising of 1745. Wesley appeals to a Protestant God to "quell Thy church's foe" (*PW,* 6:150); he never mentions the French by name, but alludes to "Ye murderers of *Rome*" and to "the *Romish* wolf " (*PW,* 6:152). Two pieces in the collection are biblical paraphrases; the first (Jeremiah 47:6–7) chastises a nation that would spurn, mock, and despise God:

> Supinely negligent and proud,
> The noble and ignoble crowd
>   In deadly slumber sleep:
> The nation sleeps, of conquest sure,
> Stands on a precipice secure,
>   Nor dreads the yawning deep.
>   (*PW,* 6:157)

In the second paraphrase (Revelation 19:11–21), Wesley calls for God to " 'Stablish Thy dominion here" (*PW*, 6:160), to

> Let the heathen fall before Thee,
> Let the isle Thy power declare;
> Judge and conquer
> All mankind in righteous war.
>
> (*PW*, 6:160)

In both poems, we may note the advantage of updating both Old and New Testaments to a specific occasion, as well as the ease by which the language of the Bible, carefully chosen, applies to contexts that generally parallel ancient events. And, of course, the familiarity of readers with those events makes the new versions significant and effective. In this manner the two major hymnodists of the eighteenth century, Isaac Watts and Charles Wesley, remained fixed to ideas and language from Scriptures in the majority of their divine poems.

In sixteen *Hymns . . . on the Thanksgiving-Day* for Hawke's victory, Wesley further cautions the British nation away from their adoration of human exploits; rather, "Our whole miraculous success / Ascribe to God alone" (*PW*, 6:163). He realizes that Britons have perhaps forgotten December 1745, when Charles Edward's force reached Derby; further, they may have forgotten that

> Jehovah then pronounced the word,
> And lo! at Thy supreme command
> The blasted savages of *Rome*
> Recoiled—and sunk into the tomb.
>
> (*PW*, 6:171)

Nonetheless, the poet questions if the defeat of the Jacobites gave rise to a new faith in God, or if the nation has only been "lull'd in more profound repose / Abused, and forfeited our peace?" (*PW*, 6:171). Throughout the volume, Wesley assumes the collective conscience of all who have neglected the worship of God, and he becomes the spokesman for those who continue to have faith in the Divine power. The real value of the thanksgiving poems, however, lies in the poet's understanding of what the recent conflict has cost in terms of human life. Despite his own personal fear and detestation of Catholic France, he realized that whatever her differences with Great Britain, both are *Christian* nations; thus, he can reduce the

entire Seven Years' War to a single line: "This waste of *Christian
blood" (PW,* 6:184). In the end, he cannot bring himself to ask
God for outright vengeance upon England's enemy; instead,

> We mourn the slaughter'd sons of *Gaul,*
> We tremble, while Thy judgments fall
>   On our invaders' head:
> Their lives to ransom ours are given,
> And crowds out of the body driven
>   Have perish'd in our stead.
>
>   *(PW,* 6:185)

And so he terminates the poems celebrating an English victory not
on a note of outright triumph, but upon one of controlled hope and
harmony:

> Repentance upon us both bestow,
> Our foes and us; that each may know
>   Their sins through faith forgiven,
> That all may cordially embrace,
> And sweetly reconciled by grace,
>   Go hand in hand to heaven.
>
>   *(PW,* 6:186)

Such are the thoughts of a religious poet, one free from political
influence and personal ambition. Integrity, if it does not always
produce great poetry, at least can give rise to clear religious expression.

Perhaps the saddest occasion prompting Charles Wesley's poetic
response was the loss of the American colonies. The final defeat of
the British at Yorktown marked both a victory for rebellious colonists and a triumph for the new nation's European ally, Catholic
France. In 1781, Wesley published *Hymns for the Nation,* a collection
of sixteen poems in two parts; he followed that with a companion
volume, *Hymns for the National Fast, Feb. 8, 1782,* containing fifteen
selections. In the twentieth century, students of history came to
realize that the loss of the thirteen American colonies did little
damage to the overall might of Great Britain. In fact, the uprising
that began in 1775, "by providing . . . useful lessons in naval and
military administration, and a healthful shock to its complacency
. . . probably strengthened Britain in the struggle that was to
come with Revolutionary France and Napoleon."[6] At the time,

however, British morale had fallen considerably; anarchy and Popery, it was believed, had won the day over the heretofore invincible triumvirate of God, King, and the Church of England. Thus we might expect verse reflecting the poet's utter despair, language lacking hope for and in the future.

At age seventy-four, Charles Wesley had abandoned neither his hope nor his faith; his commitment to Methodism had, in fact, strengthened the latter. He was prepared for "Thy severe decree" upon a nation that had forsaken God; unless Britons "to our Smiter turn, / And leave the sins for which we mourn," nothing could be salvaged from the surrender in Virginia (*PW*, 8:283–84). As Christians must give thanks to God for victories, they must also seek his forgiveness for defeat; whatever the results, all of His judgments are just. Thus Wesley established a tone for *Hymns for the Nation*. Taking his cue from *Amos* 7:2—"O Lord God, forgive, I beseech thee: by whom shall Jacob rise? for he is small"—the poet resolves the issue by claiming that

> Th' intrepid man of virtuous zeal,
> Resolved and incorruptible,
>   Who seeks our nation's good:
> Our nation's good, and not his own;
> While listening to the plaintive moan,
>   Of loyalty oppress'd,
> He serves his King's and God's designs,
> *America* and *Britain* joins,
>   And blends them in his breast.
>   (*PW*, 8:187)

From the fragments of the American Revolution have emerged, for Wesley, a lesson in political concord and peace, as well as two nations united in their praise of God through Christ. He hopes that the British monarch will no longer "By factious demagogues gainsaid, / By fawning sycophants betray'd" (*PW*, 8:295); then God will "The authors of our woes forgive, / And snatch their souls from endless woes" (*PW*, 8:295); then all despair and strife will end through the people's deliverance "Because we trust in Jesu's blood, / And ask the grace in Jesu's name" (*PW*, 8:299). Simply and forcibly, Wesley places his complete faith in the "God, who would'st a world forgive" (*PW*, 8:305). In his own mind, he can at least relieve the

pain from the most shocking setback suffered by his nation during
his lifetime.

The *Hymns for the National Fast* (1782) generalizes upon the ideas
of the earlier volume: the sin of an entire nation guilty of extreme
ungodliness. Wesley emphasizes that the loss of the American colonies—or the defeat of British arms—cannot be blamed only upon
the King, his ministers, or his soldiers. Instead, the entire nation
had turned from God: "The poor and rich, the low and high, /
Alike disdain their God to dread" (*PW*, 8:311). Each of the fifteen
poems alludes to or repeats directly the accusation. Rebellion, anarchy, French intervention, dismembered empire, tyranny, and
demagoguery: such terms move freely through Wesley's verse upon
the familiar waves of sin, insolence, crime, denial, evil, and shame.
There is bitterness in his language and chastisement in his heart;
but there also exist certain simple alternatives: renewed faith in
God, complemented by fervent prayer. Otherwise, there will be
merely an England wallowing in misery, a kingdom "wasted and
o'erthrown," a nation writhing under "showers of vengeance" from
God's "destructive work" (*PW*, 8:319). Should Britons choose to
return to faith and prayer, then the entire outlook for the nation
will assume a different image; then, the island-kingdom will blos-
som forth into what he terms "the joy unspeakable" (*PW*, 8:325).
What makes it all so possible, all so simple, is the existence of a
God "who art always the same, / Whose nature is still to forgive"
(*PW*, 8:336). How easily does Charles Wesley, once the shackles
of human sin have been cut away, fuse the political with the theological and point the way to the fundamentals of human existence:

> Concord, on a distant shore,
> To our countrymen restore;
> Every obstacle remove,
> Melt our hatred into love.
> Gospel grace to each extend,
> Every foe and every friend,
> Then in Thee we sweetly find
> Peace with God and all mankind.
>   (*PW*, 8:335)

The loss of thirteen British colonies some three thousand miles away
diminishes once the great peace has been established, both in Britain
and throughout the world.

Almost a full year before the news reached England of the defeat at Yorktown, an event of more immediate significance occurred in London that personally affected both John and Charles Wesley. As a result of the Catholic Relief Act of 1778, which saw the removal of civil restrictions against Roman Catholics in effect since William III's reign, religious intolerance intensified. In 1779, Lord George Gordon (1751–1793) assumed the presidency of the Protestant Association, formed primarily to force the repeal of the Relief Act. After presenting their petition to Parliament, the agitators, incited and led by Gordon, went off to burn Roman Catholic chapels. The days following, from 2–7 June 1780, provided examples of agitation and prejudice bringing out the basest of human reactions: prisons attacked and prisoners freed, Lord Chief Justice Mansfield's house and much of his library destroyed, the Bank of England stormed. Not until 9 June did the military manage to restore order, arresting 450 persons and hanging another twenty-five. Lord Gordon, tried for high treason, gained acquittal through the efforts of his lawyer, Thomas Erskine.

The Gordon Riots moved Charles Wesley to publish thirteen *Hymns Written in the Time of the Tumults* (1780). Certainly he had personal ties here: Gordon resided in Welbeck Street, and thus was a near neighbor; Lord Mansfield, a classmate of the poet at Westminster School, would often walk from his house in Bloomsbury Square to Chesterfield Street, Marylebone, where Wesley resided. The loss of the jurist's vast and valuable library, including works of Pope and Bolingbroke with those writers' own marginal comments, must have been a severe blow to the scholarly Wesley, especially in light of the parallel between the rioters and his father's unruly parishioners in Lincolnshire some seventy years earlier. Thus he lashes out,

> Havoc, th' infernal leader cries!
> Havoc, th' associate host replies!
> The rabble shouts, the torrent pours,
> The city sinks, the flame devours!
> (*PW*, 8:267)

Even the chapel established by John Wesley in City Road less than two years earlier appeared in danger, particularly since the Wesleys and their Methodist followers were forced, periodically, to withstand accusations of Papist sympathies. Possibly Charles Wesley's own life was threatened during that week, as evidenced by one poem in the collection entitled "Upon Notice Sent One That His House Was *Marked"*:

> In vain doth the assassin dark
> This house for desolation mark,
> Protected by the scarlet sign,
> Already mark'd with blood Divine;
> His idle threatenings we defy,
> For the destroyer *must* pass by.
>   (*PW*, 8:272)

When the riots finally subsided, Wesley, as usual, turned to give his thanks to God on behalf of the nation. The entire series of events he ascribed to devils, men, traitors, and profligates whose "ravaging fires" were ultimately "quench'd" by God's word. In the end, "Rebellion expires and peace is restored" (*PW*, 8:280).

The examples cited throughout this section are from thirteen volumes of poems wherein Charles Wesley gathered, from the important events of his day, material for public praise, thanksgiving, and even lament. The lines reflect the poet's sincere faith rising from his far-ranging loyalties and his desire to relate matters of state to Christian experience. He succeeded in communicating that faith because he sought a wide audience: he relied upon what people, especially Methodists, knew and felt, upon the essence of their own values. And he knew their prejudices and their fears—traditional and immediate, political and theological. Culturally superior to the majority of persons whom he addressed in his verse, Wesley intentionally held back the knowledge that he had accumulated and, instead, filtered his reactions to national concerns through Scripture. In his poems and hymns, he turned away from formal learning and focused upon the most familiar concentration of ideas in all of western world literature—the Bible. The difference between the occasional poetry of Charles Wesley and the mountains of political verse penned during the reign of Anne is, simply, that political poets chose to catapult important persons and events above the level of the common man, to write epics about heroes. Wesley, on the other hand, strived to familiarize, to educate his readers with the essential theological lessons associated with and derived from the occasions about which he wrote.

Religious Verse

Even the most superficial study of eighteenth-century intellectual thought brings us quickly to the realization that the major religious poets of Britain—Isaac Watts, John Newton, William Cowper, Charles Wesley—labored under the notion that they were obliged to anchor their poetry to particular passages in Scripture. The obligation, it seems, stemmed from the practice among Nonconformist and evangelical divines to relate both hymn and sermon to the same biblical text; not unlike the practice that continues to this very day, the principal function of the congregational hymn was to illustrate and support the thesis of the sermon. Thus Book I of Isaac Watts's *Hymns and Spiritual Songs* bears the title "Collected from the Holy Scriptures"; the *Olney Hymns* of William Cowper and John Newton begins with poems "On Select Texts of Scripture"; and between those two collections Charles Wesley placed his two volumes of *Short Hymns on Select Passages of Holy Scriptures.* As the principal poet of eighteenth-century evangelicalism, however, the younger Wesley had far more spiritual and poetic motivation than merely paying lip service to the proprieties of church liturgy. Indeed, the paraphrases of Scriptures, especially those pieces focusing upon the books of the Old Testament prophets, demonstrate that Charles Wesley was profoundly concerned about his own personal faith. Unlike his more traditionally minded predecessors and contemporaries, Wesley chose not to conceal his faith behind a curtain of restrained objectivity; rather, he struggled to inject his own interpretation into the important issue of prophecy, even though the results did not always provide the ultimate solutions to his own personal problems or his own spiritual unrest.

To identify the essence of Charles Wesley's spiritual unrest and to summarize the specific personal problems that produced it, we must begin with the premise that Charles, the poetic voice of British Methodism, was never really able to achieve the level of popular prominence (today the term is *exposure)* necessary for him to develop and then project a prophetic image of his own making. This in no way suggests a deep-seated jealousy of his brother John, or even the slightest degree of personal rivalry between the two. What does emerge, however, is evidence to support the observation that throughout his life, Charles Wesley existed in the shadow of his older brother, functioning as an extension of and a complement to the administration and the authority of John Wesley. Of course, one must remember that such an existence was of Charles's own choosing and making, for, as we have seen from the Oxford Holy Club venture, he was quick to recognize the superiority of John's administrative and organizational abilities over his own. He abdicated, as it were, his claim to the high priesthood of Oxford Methodism. In October 1735, the brothers embarked for Georgia; poor health forced Charles to return to England in December 1736, a full year before John's departure, abruptly ending any hope of his participation in further missionary work in America. Charles took to the paths and the highways of Great Britain well in advance of John's itinerancy, but again he drove himself to exhaustion and suffered severely from gout, the family affliction of the Wesleys. By late 1756, his strength was broken, as well as his dream of personally carrying the message for High Church reform throughout Britain. Another serious attack of gout in 1760 permanently relegated him to overseeing the London societies, and for the next twenty-eight years he labored in the suburbs of Methodist activity, his faith shaken, his leadership under constant question.[7]

The *Hymns on Select Passages of the Holy Scripture* stands as an able representative of Charles Wesley's religious verse, and it constitutes the poet's first major collection following the termination of his period of itinerancy. On the one hand, the effort proved the result of sound theological advice, encouragement, and precedence, gathered from a lifetime of sources ranging from Paul's epistle to the Hebrews, through Isaac Watts's paraphrases of Psalms, to John Wesley's own *Explanatory Notes on the New Testament*, in addition to the commentaries of Robert Gell, Matthew Henry, and Johannes Albrecht Bengel.[8] On the other hand, the *Short Hymns* sounded the opening note of the prophet whose voice—whose *prophecy*, as it were—would have to be channeled, from then on, through his poetry. Garbed, for the moment, in the heavy mantle of Isaiah, he pleads,

> Send forth one ray of heavenly light,
>   Of gospel-hope, or humble fear,
> To guide me through this gulf of night,
>   My poor, desponding soul to cheer,

> Till Thou mine unbelief remove,
> And show me all Thy glorious love.
> (*PW*, 9:420)

And so, in this major work, the bard of British Methodism set down no less than 2,030 poetic paraphrases[9] in an effort to prove, both to himself and to tens of thousands of Methodists, that "*Heathens* and *Jews* through Jesus join, / And God and Man in Christ are one" (*PW*, 10:138). The attempts to substantiate that thesis, to fulfill that prophecy, become most emphatic in the 563 paraphrases of the Old Testament prophetic books.

Perhaps the one obvious quality of the prophetic paraphrases in the *Short Hymns on Select Passages of the Holy Scripture* lies in Wesley's ability to manipulate Old Testament language, theme, and context, while building upon Old Testament analogies. For instance, when the prophet Hosea narrates the tragedy of his marriage to the unfaithful Gomer in terms of compassionate yearning, he simultaneously reveals God's true feeling for the Israelite nation:

Therefore, behold, I will allure her, and bring her unto the wilderness, and speak comfortably unto her. And I will give her vineyards from thence, and the valley of Achor for a door of hope: and she shall sing there, as in the days of her youth, and as in the day when she came up out of the land of Egypt.   (2:14–15)[10]

As a religious poet, as a hymnodist, Wesley takes full advantage of the form with which he works. The two verses from Hosea 2 yield, technically, four poems (*PW*, 10:73–74, Hymns 1431–34); yet, we might well mount an argument in favor of a single, clearly unified poetic piece. In a congregational sense, he has no need for Gomer and what she represents; rather, in the first piece (#1431), he directs the worshiper to "Sing to the God of faithful love! / His goodness and His truth we prove . . ." (*PW*, 10:73). "I will allure her into the wilderness" becomes *we* (as Christian worshipers and Christian singers) having been "Allured into the wilderness" (Hymn 1431, l. 3), a sentiment that opens the second poem:

> Allured into the desert
> Of trouble and temptation,
>   Again we hear
>   The Comforter,

The God of our salvation:
(Hymn 1432, ll. 1–5)

The key to Charles Wesley's four poems appears, at the outset, not
really that far removed from Hosea's prophecy. Both original and
paraphrase focus upon God's yearning for His chosen people; there
is hope for those people now, just as there was hope when God
brought them out of Egypt. The difference, of course, is that Wesley, although perfectly willing to be towed along by the combination
of Old Testament nature imagery and Miltonic oxymoron—"Here
in the depth of sweet distress / Again our vineyards we possess, /
And drink the dead-reviving wine:" (Hymn 1433, ll. 1–3)—never
loses sight of his role as hymnodic prophet of eighteenth-century
evangelicalism. His Israelites rush pell-mell out of Egypt, "shouting
our Redeemer's name, / Triumphant pass'd the parted flood" (Hymn
1434, ll. 506–7), to be embraced by the outstretched arms of
Christianity and, at the end of the fourth and final hymn from Hosea
2, the fulfillment of Hosea's prophecy:

> Jesus the Lord again we sing,
> Who did us to salvation bring,
>   And now repeats our sins forgiven;
> We now His glorious Spirit breathe,
> Tread down the fear of Hell and Death,
>   And live on earth the life of heaven.
>   (Hymn 1434, ll. 7–12)

Of course, Wesley has done nothing radical or controversial, except,
perhaps, to demonstrate his thorough knowledge of Scriptures. Ever
so skillfully, without attracting too much attention (notice line 9
in the quotation immediately preceding), he reminded worshipers
of the numerous echoes from Old Testament prophecy reverberating
throughout New Testament gospels and epistles. His line, "And
now repeats our sins forgiven," bridges, both for himself and for
the Christian worshiper whom he addressed, the theological and
chronological gaps between Hosea's "For I desired mercy, and not
sacrifice" (6:16) and Christ's "I will have mercy, and not sacrifice:
for I am not come to call the righteous, but sinners to repentance"
(Matthew 9:13).

The prophecy of hope, as filtered through the analogy of Hosea's
supposedly misguided wife, relate significantly to certain problems

experienced by the prophet Jeremiah. In the midst of the gloom brought on by the Babylonian domination of the Israelites, Jeremiah claims that the people of Judah and Israel will, eventually, regain their land. At first, he announces how "The Lord hath appeared of old unto me, *saying*, Yea, I have loved thee with an everlasting love: therefore, with lovingkindness I have drawn thee" (Jeremiah 31:3). For both Jeremiah *and* Charles Wesley, the trauma of the struggling prophet—lonely, unpopular, compelled by a dual loyalty to his people and to his God—can be transformed to the dilemma of the struggling sinner:

> Draw me, Saviour, from above,
>   Still to every sin inclined,
> Bind me with the cords of love;
>   Love alone my soul can bind.
> Stop its vile propensity,
>   Change its groveling appetite,
> Jesus, manifest to me,
>   By Thyself my pure delight.
> (*PW*, 10:36, Hymn 1342,
>   ll. 1–8)

After purging himself of his inner pessimism by having the full opportunity to feel sorry for himself, Jeremiah then turns his attention specifically to the restoration of the people to the land. Their sorrow fades before the usual, but still powerful, instruments of God and nature: ". . . they shall come and sing . . . and shall flow together to the goodness of the Lord, for wheat, and for wine, and for oil, and for the young of the flock and of the herd; and their soul shall be as a watered garden; and they shall not sorrow any more at all" (Jeremiah 31:12). Then the prophet sounds, upon the instrument of hope, the note of eventual restoration: "And there is hope in thine end . . . that thy children shall come again to their own border" (Jeremiah 31:17).

As both a writer of religious verse and a student of the Bible, Charles Wesley could appreciate the fine line between the necessarily somber, prophetic tone of the passage from Scriptures and the exuberance or religious positivism represented by eighteenth-century congregational song. For Wesley, that fine line constituted the essence of the evangelical hymn; thus, even during his own bouts with dejection, he pressed forward to penetrate the dense gloom of the Babylonian captivity enshrouding Jeremiah and his people:

> Sing, ye happy souls that press
> Toward the height of holiness,
> Praise Him whom in part ye know,
> Freely to his goodness flow,
> All His promises receive,
> All the grace He hath to give.
> (*PW*, 10:37, Hymn 1344,
> ll. 1–6)

With the exception of the excitement, the anticipation generating from the piece, Wesley remains fairly well fixed to Jeremiah's prophetic imagery, although the Methodist poet does expand it to focus upon "the living Bread," "the unction from above," "the Oil of Joy, and wine of love" (10:37, Hymn 1344, ll. 9–12). The "watered garden" image receives the heaviest emphasis from Wesley, as he equates the theme of restoration of the land with the reclamation, by man, of God's terrestrial paradise. Again, he fills the air with song—*congregational* song—to demonstrate that "Quite recover'd from our fall, / [we] Shall not sin or grieve at all . . ." (*PW*, 10:37–38, Hymn 1345, ll. 9–10).

The short, single poem on Jeremiah 31:17 shifts its point of view from the collective "thy children" of the Old Testament to the more personal "I":

> I take Thee at Thy word:
> Let it accomplished be:
> According to Thy promise Lord,
> In death remember me!
> O seal it on my heart;
> And when I life resign,
> My hope if in my end Thou art,
> Thou are for ever mine.
> (*PW*, 10:38, Hymn
> 1347, ll. 1–8)

Wesley comes terribly close to announcing the fulfillment of the prophecy, or at least to proclaiming that the hope of the people for reclaiming what they have lost has indeed blossomed. However, whereas Jeremiah points toward a new day for *all* of God's chosen people, Charles Wesley concentrates upon the return, after life, of the soul to God. Thus Wesley views restoration in terms not of the Old Testament political context (the nation being restored to the promised land), but of Christ's redemption: the soul being *reclaimed*, through Christ, by God.

Perhaps one of the best opportunities for Wesley to translate the Old Testament promise of restoration into the characteristic optimism of a Christian poem occurs at the end of the brief but highly poetic book of Zephaniah. The final chapter focuses upon the city of Jerusalem and the prophet's announcement of its desolation, followed by the declaration that the survivors will begin a *new* Israel. Zephaniah concludes with the vision of the happy day, wherein God will heal all afflictions, bring the people back to their land, and restore their pride in themselves as a nation under the mercy and grace of their rightful Lord (3:19–20). Wesley's prophetic imagination conjures forth two possibilities here. As a Christian and a loyal Briton, the poet sought opportunities to demonstrate the political and social benefits of Methodism in terms of its contribution to the national interest; at the same time, he kept sight of the spiritual advantages to those who chose to wrap themselves in the banner of the evangelical revival. Thus—

> Gather the nations in that day,
>   The once-distinguish'd flock bring in:
> Our old oppressive tyrants slay,
>   With all the brood of imbred sin;
> Our weak, degenerate souls forgive;
>   Where 'er we have been put to shame,
> Thy people's dignity retrieve,
>   And vindicate the Christian name.
> (*PW*, 10:108; Hymn 1527, ll. 1–8)

The other possibility for the restoration motif in Zephaniah manifests itself in the usual Wesleyan adaptation of the prophetic message. Simply, the vision of the happy day fits comfortably with the concept of the *ideal* Christian church—a Church of England strengthened by spiritual positivism and social direction, reformed from within by such movements as Wesleyan Methodism, armed morally and socially to parry such corrosive elements as Protestant Dissent and Roman Catholicism:

Collected, perfected in one,
Jesus, Thy sinless people show,
And through the wondering world make known
Thy glorious, spotless church below:
(*PW*, 10:108, Hymn 1528, ll. 1–4)

Paraphrase of Isaiah

The discussion of Charles Wesley's poetic/hymnodic Christianization of Old Testament prophecy, as well as the adaptation of that prophecy to his own personal mood and temper, cannot proceed too much further before it must come to rest upon the major prophet and the major prophetic book, Isaiah. Wesley wrote 225 poetic paraphrases of Isaiah, working especially hard to capture both the personality of the prophet and the essence of his reforms. With no less vigor, he attempted to translate those qualities into the form and style of eighteenth-century congregational song. Of course, the frequent references and allusions in the New Testament to the initial Old Testament prophetic book simplified his task, or, at least, lightened the burdens of transition. At any rate, as long as Wesley did not lose sight of his intended audience, his poetic Christianization and personal undertones made sense. Therefore, the opening address of the book announces, in somewhat threatening tones, that "I have nourished and brought up children, and they have rebelled against me" (1:2). Apparently Wesley's intent is to emphasize the special relationship between the Israelites and their God; in fact, the imagery that immediately follows—"The ox knoweth his owner, and the ass his master's crib" (1:3)—leaves no doubt as to the origin of any prophecy or covenant. For Wesley, the special relationship points to a different emphasis, one "Mark'd with the new, the Christian name. . . ." The poet translates the sound and the sense of the Old Testament political term *rebelled* into a force that destroys, in a purely *spiritual* sense, the very core of Christian love:

. . . the base degenerate seed
Impatient to divulge their shame,
Their foul ingratitude to prove,
Have spurned the bowels of My love.
(*PW*, 9:369, Hymn 1046, ll. 7–12)

A dominant quality of Charles Wesley's religious verse, whether seen in the *Short Hymns on Select Passages of Scripture* or elsewhere, is the poet's chastisement of his followers when they fail to live up to Christian principles and Christian expectations. Language such as "foul ingratitude" may indeed exist as parts of scriptural or prophetic lexicons, but it hardly belongs to such forms as the congregational song, where in fact it rarely appears. Essentially, the existence of those epithets ought, in Wesley's case, to be termed *Methodization* of Old Testament prophecy, rather than Christianization.

Undoubtedly, then, Charles Wesley performed at his best—as poet, as imitator, as biblical scholar and translator, as a true prophet of the eighteenth-century evangelical revival and its doctrine—when he could make full use of the emotions generating from the principal themes within a major prophetic book. One such theme is the glory of redeemed Zion in terms of a new creation. In *Isaiah*, God will create "new heavens and a new earth: and the former shall not be remembered, nor come into mind" (65:17). For Wesley, the verse becomes a rhymed hymn of thirty lines, whereby, initially, the congregation longingly awaits the fulfillment of the prophecy:

> Now our universe create
> Fair, beyond its first estate,
> When Thine eye with pleasure view'd,
> When Thy lips pronounced it good,
> Ruin'd now by sin and cursed,
> Speak it fairer than at first.
> (*PW*, 9:461, Hymn 1257,
>   ll. 7–12)

After observing God's "Triumph in a world of grace" and antici-pating His ultimate glory, the collective *we*, the Sons of God, come to the new Jerusalem; caught up in the realization that the new creation is upon them, they "Tell the wonders of Thy grace, / Shout Thine everlasting praise" (*PW*, 9:462, Hymn 1257, ll. 18, 25, 29–30).

The "new heavens and the new earth" appear once more in Isaiah, almost at the very end of the book (66:22). In his final poetic paraphrase of the book, Wesley finds a more practical use for the creation prophecy—more practical in terms of his eighteenth-century Christian audience. Simply, the hope held forth and explicated

by him and his brother comes to fruition, albeit in a strictly literary
sense, at this point in the *Short Hymns*. The second (and the final)
stanza of the last poem paraphrasing Isaiah reads,

> A Church which may remain
> With all Thy works restored,
> Commensurate with time, obtain
> The nature of her Lord;
> A Church to comprehend
> The whole of human race,
> And live in joys that never end
> Before Thy glorious face.
> (*PW*, 9:471, Hymn 1271,
> ll. 9–16)

Here, then, lies the true purpose of Wesleyan Methodism. Neither
of the Wesleys advocated withdrawal from the Established Church,
an act that would, at that particular time, have turned one of the
major religious and social movements of eighteenth-century England
into nothing more than another insignificant and weak limb of
Protestant Dissent. Indeed, both the leader and the laureate of
Methodism sought the "Church which may remain"—an Anglican
church, a church into which they had both been ordained, a church
reformed from within and through the efforts of its own agents, "A
Church to comprehend / The whole of human race. . . ." Unfortunately, the separation would occur, almost immediately following
John Wesley's death in the first week of March 1791; thirty years
earlier, however, Charles Wesley could alleviate his own discontent
by placing his confidence in the glory enunciated through Isaiah's
prophecy.

Paraphrases of Lamentations and Minor Prophets

Obviously, while there exist expressions of hope and joy in Old
Testament prophecy, there may also be found the agonizing sobs
of suffering and disappointment. Consider, for instance, the highly
grief-stricken tone—yet, at the same time, the highly poetic structure—of Lamentations, as the prophet moves from the expression
of his grief over the general desolation of Israel to his recollection
of God's love as the basis for hope. Further, he progresses through
those themes upon the standard Old Testament conveyances of ex-

hortation to repentance, confession, and prayer. The prophet's misery may be viewed through his frustration, as when he bewails, "Is it nothing to you, all ye that pass by? behold, and see if there be any sorrow like unto my sorrow, which is done unto me, wherewith the Lord hath afflicted *me* in the day of his fierce anger" (1:12). Then, adopting momentarily the tone of the psalmist, the lamenting prophet allows for a thin ray of hope:

> It is good for a man that he bear the yoke in his youth.
> He sitteth alone and keepeth silence, because he hath borne it upon him.
> He putteth his mouth in the dust; if so be there may be hope.
> (3:27–29)

Nevertheless, the mood of suffering sustains itself, even to the final section of the book, as the prophet bewails the fact that "The crown is fallen *from* our head: woe unto us, that we have sinned!" (5:16).

Charles Wesley certainly observed the suffering and the disappointment stamped clearly upon the pages of Lamentations, and he was not insensitive to either. In his view, however, there remained the drive "to prove and . . . guard the doctrine of Christian perfection" (*PW*, 9:vii), and he moved quickly to transcend the spiritual and the physical burdens of the Old Testament prophet by creating, in their place, a mood of definite Christian positivism. The twelfth verse of the first chapter ("It is nothing to you") immediately conjures forth visions of Christ on the Cross; Wesley steps in to give substance to that suggestion: the narrator of his short paraphrase, having never "stopp'd on *Calvary*," knew nothing of what that scene actually meant for him; but then he realizes that the "bleeding cross" is the symbol of man's hope. "To me Thy death is life, Thy loss / Is mine eternal gain" (*PW*, 10:508 Hymn 1367, ll. 1–2). The strength, the substance of that hope, gathers an even greater degree of positivism when viewed within the same context as the Old Testament, namely the mouth-in-the-dust setting. Although Wesley's singer-narrator may sit silent and alone (as does the prophet), and though he may humble himself in the dirt (as does the prophet), he will eventually find considerably more than the mere *promise* of a new world. To the contrary, the tone is definitely positive as Wesley's narrator will see the Son of God "merciful and just," as well as "Joyful in affliction . . ." (*PW*, 10:50, Hymn 1574, ll.

14–15). Wesley then concludes his paraphrase of Lamentations by paying only token service to the final notes of the prophet's cry of woe. The singer of his songs knows the "cause of all my sad distress" and feels the "meaning of this pain"; nevertheless, instead of a negative mood of rejection, he bursts forth into a shout of exuberant renewal. Able to toss aside "This root of bitterness," Wesley's narrator announces his soul to "be life and peace / And pure eternal joy" (*PW*, 10:52, Hymn 1359, ll. 2, 7, 14, 17–18). Therefore, by the end of the paraphrase of both the single verse and the complete Old Testament book, Wesley has practically purged his reader of the Hebrew prophet's plea for deliverance from tribulation; indeed, the poet himself has created a totally different atmosphere of deliverance, one supported by firm Christian doctrine.

Scholars have concluded, generally, that Charles Wesley wrote religious verse in quantity so that he could supply substance for Christian teaching and public praise, as well as give some degree of objectivity to his own personal belief.[11] Certainly, no argument can be found with Wesley's determination to inject substance into Christian teaching and public worship; the question does arise, however, as to whether he could objectify his own faith. On the surface, we may observe that a poet thoroughly committed to his religion, as well as being deeply affected by a full range of moods, would be able to set forth generalizations for a number and variety of congregations, both present and future. But Charles Wesley was never quite able to do that; instead, a relatively clear prophetic statement such as ". . . by the blood of thy covenant I have sent forth thy prisoners out of the pit wherein there *is* no water" (Zechariah 9:11) becomes a statement of deep personal trauma:

> Out of the pit of sin I cry,
>   Sinking into the pit of hell,
> Till Thou that covenant blood apply,
>   And bid my heart the comfort feel;
> Speak, Father, speak the gracious word,
>   Which makes the dying sinner live,
> Send forth the prisoner of the Lord,
>   And now for Jesu's sake forgive.
>   (*PW*, 10:119, Hymn 1559, ll. 1–8)

Despite the apparent surface objectivity of the form with which he works, Charles Wesley cannot hide behind the collective voice of the congregational hymn, as no poet can remove himself, effectively or entirely, from his lines. The Old Testament prophetic echo may have been, potentially, a good hiding place for Wesley's troubled soul, since prophetic echoes reverberated from the collective conscience of the entire nation. Even the Christianization process, the obvious means for carrying out the Christian teaching phase of his overall purpose, does not obscure the personal utterance, the traumatic pleas, of the deeply unsettled heart. In the end, Old Testament prophecy, seasoned with liberal doses of Christian fulfillment for the benefit of thousands of unsophisticated adherents to the new evangelicalism, serves as the essence of the Methodist poet's paraphrases. Charles Wesley, as poet and as writer of congregational hymns, could indeed agree with the prophet Micah (4:5) that "all people will walk every one in the name of his god"; Charles Wesley, devout, insecure, and troubled—but, nevertheless a Christian—needed something more direct and personal. Through his own art, his own personal expression, he found and then explicated the prophecy that he really needed, the prophecy from which he could derive real help and guidance. Thus—

> Determined I am
> Through Jesus's grace,
> To walk in His name,
> To walk in His ways,
> With constant endeavour
> To practise His word,
> And own Him for ever
> My God and my Lord.
> (*PW*, 10:96, Hymn 1492, ll. 1–8)

Conclusion

Although Charles Wesley's religious verse reflects the influence of a variety of British poets, ranging from the Elizabethan Shakespeare to the Augustan Edward Young, we have seen that both the sound and the sense of Scripture remained his principal sources. Thus, in a piece entitled "Waiting for the Promise" (from *Hymns and Sacred Poems*, 1742), we may observe—

> Fainting soul, be bold, be strong;
>   Wait the leisure of thy Lord:
> Though it seem to tarry long,
>   True and faithful in His word.   (*PW*, 2:293)

Wesley's contemporaries would have recognized the words of Psalm 27:16 from Miles Coverdale's prose version in the *Book of Common Prayer*: "O tarry thou the Lord's leisure," indicating that Methodism's bard continued to hold firm to his Anglican upbringing and to his Anglican education. Yet, the younger Wesley must not be thought of as a mere paraphraser of Scripture, a versifier who simply combined experience with emotionalism and who very carefully injected both into the liturgy of the Methodist service. Instead, he deserves recognition as a legitimate, devotional poet who established the notion that the congregational hymn is indeed a poem, a divine ode intended for public expression. John Wesley, in the preface to *A Collection of Hymns for the Use of the People Called Methodists* (1780), set forth what still stands as the most accurate assessment of his brother's poetry: "In these hymns there is no doggerel, no botches, nothing to put in to patch the rhyme, no feeble expletives. . . . Here are . . . both the purity, the strength and the elegance of the ENGLISH language: and at the same time the utmost simplicity and plainness, suited to every capacity." The patriarch of the Methodists challenged critics of the age to judge "whether there is not in some of the following verses, the true Spirit of Poetry: such as cannot be acquired by art and labour; but must be the gift of nature." He concluded that through labor "a man may become a tolerable imitator. . . . But unless he is born a Poet, he will never attain the genuine SPIRIT OF POETRY."[12]

Despite his brother's exuberance, Charles Wesley met with only limited success and acceptance outside of the boundaries of Methodism. Today, there is wide poetic and hymnodic acceptance of such pieces as "All praise to Him who dwells in bliss"; "Christ the Lord is risen today"; "Christ, whose glory fills the sky"; "Come, let us join our friends above"; "Come, Thou long-expected Jesus"; "Hail the day that sees Him rise"; "Hark! how all the welkin sings"; "Hark, the herald angels sing"; "Lo! He comes, with clouds descending"; "Love Divine, all loves excelling"; "Jesu, Lover of my soul." By the middle of the eighteenth century, however, English congregational song had been nurtured by the common meters and generalized experiences from the voices of Protestant Dissent: Isaac Watts, Philip Doddridge, Thomas Gibbons, and Joseph Hart. Wesley's *specific* experiences, his departure from the simple meters of the old Psalmody, his enthusiastic and controversial but nevertheless controlled spirit—all appeared foreign to the tastes of those congregations unfamiliar with the influences and the teachings of Wesleyan Methodism.

Not until late in the nineteenth century, when Methodism finally emerged from the abuse and scorn of contemporary rivals, did Charles Wesley's devotional poetry achieve the recognition due it. Essentially, the major pieces were seen to reflect the poet's sincere faith arising from his far-ranging loyalties and his desire to interpret Christian experience. His poetry emerged, for him, as a compromise between the intellect and the faith, as he relied upon what he believed people knew and felt and reached down to the very core of their own values. Culturally superior to the majority of persons whom he addressed, Charles Wesley intentionally held back his own knowledge; instead, he wove his reactions and concerns through Scriptures, attempting, like his brother John, to educate his readers with essential doctrinal lessons. In the end, there remains little doubt as to the purpose and direction of a new voice who spoke with and for certain eighteenth-century Britons seeking God in times of trouble:

> Weary of all this wordy strife,
> These notions, forms, and modes, and names,
> To Thee, the Way, the Truth, the Life,
> Whose love my simple heart inflames,
> Divinely taught, at last, I fly,
> With Thee, and Thine to live, and die.
> (*PW*, 6:71)

Chapter Five

Sermons and Religious Prose Tracts

Sermons

From the outset, we must distinguish between John Wesley the preacher of sermons and Wesley the writer of sermons, since we are really faced with the problem of two different items. Although he kept careful accounts—in the diaries, journal, and Sermon Register[1]—of the sources upon which he based his pulpit addresses, Wesley was, essentially, an extemporaneous speaker. There lies within the warehouse of Wesleyana a report of an incident (part of which he records in the journals) on 28 December 1788, when an aged John Wesley preached a sermon at Allhallows Church, Lombard Street, London,[2] for the benefit of forty-eight poor children of the St. Ethelburga Society. While putting on his gown, Wesley remarked to the attendant that more than fifty years had passed since he had first preached at Allhallows. He told the man about the earlier occasion, when

I came without a sermon; and going up the pulpit stairs, I hesitated, and returned into the vestry under much mental confusion and agitation. A woman who stood by, noticed my concern, and said, "Pray, sir, what is the matter?" I replied, "I have not brought a sermon with me." Putting her hand on my shoulder, she said, "Is that all? Cannot you trust God for a sermon?" The question had such an effect upon me, that I ascended the pulpit, preached extempore, with great freedom to myself, and acceptance to the people; and have never since taken a written sermon into the pulpit.[3]

The anecdote serves as a means for separating Wesley the orator from Wesley the writer and makes clear that what we have read in numerous editions of the sermons was prepared for the *press,* not for

74

the pulpit. The substance of the two may well have been the same, but the method, the style, and the tone of the printed versions are simply too controlled, too polished, too fine to have been "preached extempore."

Wesley himself, in the earliest collection of his pulpit oratory (*Sermons on Several Occasions*. 3 vols., 1746), identified the overall guiding purpose of his sermon texts: "I want to know one thing, the way to heaven: how to land safe on that happy shore. God himself has condescended to teach the way; for this very end he came from heaven. He hath written it down in a book! Oh give me that book! At any price, give me the book of God! I have it: here is knowledge enough for me. Let me be *homo unius libri*."[4] Thus, when he prepared to publish the sermons, both individually and collectively, he revised and arranged them with a view toward emphasizing the differences between the ways of God and the ways of men. And, as always, the ways are paved with a simple and direct style: a mixture of clear language, easily discernible scriptural allusion, and a tirade of rhetorical questioning:

> Does the love of God constrain thee to serve Him with fear,—to "rejoice unto him with reverence?" Art thou more afraid of displeasing God, than either of death or hell? Is nothing so terrible to thee as the thought of offending the eyes of his glory? Upon this ground, dost thou "hate all evil ways," every transgression of his holy and perfect law; and herein "exercise thyself to have a conscience void of offence towards God, and towards man?" ("Catholic Spirit" [1:351])

If, in the Miltonic sense, Wesley fuels his sermons with biblical energy "to justify the ways of God to men," he is at least equally concerned with justifying the ways of Methodism to eighteenth-century Britons. The printed texts, widely circulated during their author's lifetime, became heralds by which John Wesley determined to promote "this scriptural, primitive religion." He pleads, at the end of the sermon dedicating the foundation of City Road Chapel (21 April 1777), to "diffuse the religion of love among all we have any intercourse with: let us provoke all men, not to enmity and contention, but to love and to good works . . ." (1:498). But he is not so taken up with promoting his cause that he forgets to pay service to those simple rhetorical modes that will temper his exuberance with reason. In the same address, he pauses a third of the

way through to define his key term: "Methodism," he claims, "is
the old religion, the religion of the Bible, the religion of the primitive church, the religion of the Church of England. This old religion
. . . is no other than love, the love of God and of all mankind
. . ." (1:493). The definition emerges as the final point in the
introduction to the argument; in the preceding ten paragraphs,
Wesley has carefully framed the history of his movement, beginning
with his undergraduate studies at Christ Church and moving forward
to the establishment of the London societies and then to the work
of Methodism in Cornwall, Wales, Ireland, and Scotland. The sermon may be cited as an example of how well Wesley can turn an
address for the dedication of a building—albeit a *Methodist* building—into an opportunity to outline the rise and progress of "primitive religion" in Britain. Again, however, it is important to
remember that the result, although perhaps intended to reach the
ears of a congregation, is *not* pulpit oratory. Instead, Wesley has
given his congregation of readers a fully developed prose essay.

    Further proof of the care with which Wesley constructed his
published sermons can be seen through analyses of two addresses
rising from rather important occasions, both concerning the same
underlying theme: death. The first resulted from the death of George
Whitefield at Newburyport, Massachusetts, on 30 September 1770.
Although he and Wesley had differed radically on their views concerning Anglican and Methodist doctrine and on such a social issue
as slavery, and although they had quarreled personally on more than
one occasion, time and mutual respect had returned them to the
point of coexistence. Whitefield in fact had made arrangements for
Wesley to preach his funeral sermon at the Tabernacle in Moorfields
and in the Chapel at Tottenham Court Road, the two citadels of
the Calvinist Methodists. Thus, upon returning to London on 10
November from Norwich and hearing of his rival's death, Wesley
spent the next seven days at Lewisham at work on the sermons to
be delivered on Sunday, the eighteenth.[5]

    For his biblical text, Wesley turned to Numbers, the fourth of
the Old Testament books ascribed to Moses, containing the experiences of the Hebrews from their second year in the wilderness to
their arrival on the borders of Moab, close to the promised land.
Specifically, he extracts the words of the magician Balaam (23:10):
"Let me die the death of the righteous, and let my last end be like
his!" With the second half of that sentence, he begins the sermon,

then proceeds immediately to a question: "How many of you join in this wish?" (1:471). But like Shakespeare's Antony, Wesley will not read the will; he withdraws the question, claiming the pursuit of its answer would "detain you too long from the sadly pleasing thought of your beloved brother, friend, and pastor; yea, and father, too . . ." (1:471). He moves quickly out of the two paragraphs of introduction and into the first and longest section: eighteen paragraphs wherein he traces the life and thought of his subject. Wesley, however, has little to say about Whitefield's activities in England; the largest portion emphasizes the field-preacher's conquests and conversions in America, where he had posed absolutely no threat to the ideas or to the organization of Wesleyan Methodism. Such information, we are told, was taken from Whitefield's journals, and Wesley obviously felt free to add embellishments for the occasion. Thus, in America, "the greater part of the hearers were affected to an amazing degree. Many were deeply convinced of their lost state; many truly converted to God. In some places thousands cried out aloud; many as in the agonies of death; most were drowned in tears; some turned pale as death; others were wringing their hands; others lying on the ground; others sinking into the arms of their friends; almost all lifting up their eyes, and calling for mercy" (1:473).

Upon concluding the biographical section, Wesley has completed one half of his sermon. He proceeds to consider the second and third sections, on Whitefield's character (nine paragraphs) and on how people may derive meaning and profit from Whitefield's death (ten paragraphs). He keeps the second section under tight rein by identifying, *seriatim,* those qualities which he himself observed "from a personal knowledge of near forty years": gratitude, friendship, modesty, frankness, openness, courage and intrepidity, steadiness, and integrity. Although the qualities themselves are important, and are presented clearly (though stiffly) and without any undue emphasis, Wesley saves the emotional thrust of this section for what he terms their "foundation"—their source:

. . . it was no other than faith in a bleeding Lord; faith of the operation of God. It was a lively hope of an inheritance incorruptible, undefiled, and that fadeth not away. It was the love of God shed abroad in his heart by the Holy Ghost which was given into him, filling his soul with tender, disinterested love to every child of man. (1:476–77)

Once again, he calls upon the ideas and the language of Scripture to give some substance to what really has developed into a compendium of polite epithets piled upon the tomb of a noteworthy missionary.

Only in the last section of the sermon—the final ten paragraphs—does Wesley appear comfortable with his subject. Here, he proposes to discover the real meaning behind Whitefield's death and the lessons that those whom he left behind may learn from it. The thesis now shifts to what he terms Whitefield's "grand scriptural doctrines," the essence of which is "Give God all the glory of whatever is good in man, . . . and set Christ as high and man as low as possible" (1:477). He pursues the point for another six or seven paragraphs, but adds nothing new to what his audience already knows. Nevertheless, because of its directness and its sincerity, Wesley has written an effective sermon, a moving address that contains the proper additives of reason and scriptural evidence. The climax occurs when he urges the listeners/readers to

. . . put ye on, as the elect of God, bowels of mercies, humbleness of mind, brotherly kindness, gentleness, long suffering, forbearing one another in love. Let the time past suffice for strife, envy, contention; for biting and devouring one another. Blessed be God, that ye have not long ago been consumed one of another! From hence-forth hold ye the unity of the Spirit in the bond of peace.   (1:480)

Despite the specific occasion for which his words were intended, Wesley adds the funeral sermon for George Whitefield to his collection of definitions for Methodism. It exists as another of his evangelical documents, an indirect attack upon irrational religion and a carefully understated defense of the principle that reason and religion must continue to complement each other.

The second sermon entitled "National Sins and Miseries" and preached on 12 November 1775, at St. Matthew's, Bethnal Green, is approximately one-half the size (twenty-one paragraphs) of the address for Whitefield's funeral. Both the subtitle of the sermon and the journal entry for that date tell us that Wesley preached on Sunday, 12 November, for the benefit of the widows and orphans of British soldiers who had been killed at Bunker Hill. We are told also that "Knowing how many would seek occasion of offence, I wrote down my sermon."[6] Thus, his listeners had occasion to observe

Wesley preaching from a prepared text (although he no doubt revised it before publication), prompted, as he indicated, by his own position relative to the American revolution: he was in no way disloyal to England; he simply could not bring himself to support a war that he believed England could not win.[7]

Wesley based his address on 2 Samuel 24:17, "Lo, I have sinned, and I have done wickedly; but these sheep, what have they done?" Thus he devotes the first five paragraphs to complex explications of 2 Samuel 24 and of 1 Chronicles 21, both of which lead to the conclusion that "God frequently punishes a people for the sins of their rulers; because they are generally partakers of their sins, in one kind or another" (1:515). The conclusion itself raises the question, "Is there not, in several respects, a remarkable resemblance between the case of Israel and our own?" (1:516). Within the space of two paragraphs, Wesley repeats the key passage from 2 Samuel— "Lo, I have sinned. . . ."—which leads us to the realization that he has determined to place the issue of the widows and orphans of fallen British soldiers into a larger context.

Without doubt, Wesley's sermon at St. Matthew's exists as an eloquent summary of his belief in the folly of a war with the American colonists: the inability of England to supply an army three thousand miles from its native shores, combined with the absurdity of stripping the nation of its defenses, other than ineffective militia, with which to ward off invasion by France or Spain or merely to deal with internal uprisings. And so, for the benefit of those assembled before him, he traces the current deplorable state of the nation: loss of trade and property, unemployment (particularly throughout the west and in Cornwall), want of food and raiment, and the general distrust of government. Then, as though remembering, suddenly, the tragedy of the occasion upon which he was asked to speak, Wesley attacks the source of this sin and misery:

And, as if all . . . were not miserable enough, see . . . the fell monster war! But who can describe the complicated misery which is contained in this? Hark! the cannon's roar! A pitchy cloud covers the face of the sky. Noise, confusion, terror, reign over all. Dying groans are on every side. The bodies of men are pierced, torn, hewed in pieces: their blood is poured on the earth like water! Their souls take their flight into the eternal world; perhaps into everlasting misery. The ministers of grace turn away from the horrid scene; the ministers of vengeance triumph. Such already has been the face of things in that once happy land, where peace and plenty,

even while banished from a great part of Europe, smiled for near a hundred
years.   (1:518)

The real villains of Wesley's melodramatic outburst (which appears
as a combination from Homer and the Last Judgment) are anarchy
and confusion masquerading under the banner of liberty, leaving
behind them the disconsolate widows and desolate orphans of the
fallen.

Certainly, the theme of the sermon aimed directly at the passions.
Wesley discarded most of the modes that controlled his sermon on
George Whitefield, since there was little one could do about that
event but learn from it. Bunker Hill, however, represented only
the first of what would obviously become a series of similar events
with similar outcomes. Nevertheless, the Methodist leader, while
interested in arousing the emotions of his hearers, to excite them,
still assumed responsibility for providing direction for their passions.
The real dilemma for Wesley centers upon his knowledge that in
response to his earlier, reasonable appeals to supposedly reasonable
men, he had received nothing! Thus, convinced he is dealing with
a nation of sinners—yet sinners for whom he continues to hold out
some hope—he reaches for the hearts of his congregation and offers
his listeners, at the very end of the sermon, a means by which to
halt the plague ravaging England and America:

Show mercy more especially to the poor widows, to the helpless orphans
of your countrymen, who are now numbered among the dead, who fell
among the slain in a distant land. Who knoweth but the Lord will yet
be entreated, will calm the madness of the people, will quench the flames
of contention, and breathe into all the spirit of love, unity, and concord.
Then brother shall not lift up sword against brother, neither shall they
know war any more. Then shall plenty and peace flourish in our land,
and all the inhabitants of it be thankful for the innumerable blessings
which they enjoy, and shall "fear God, and honour the king."   (1:521)

It is indeed interesting to observe, in the light of our discussion
in the preceding chapter of Charles Wesley's reaction to the end of
the American war, the close proximity of thought, method, and
solution between the two brothers. At the risk of some repetition,
we may look again at the last half of Charles Wesley's "Poem for
Peace," as it appears in *Hymns for the National Fast, Feb. 8, 1782*
(1782):

Every stubborn spirit bow,
Turn us, Lord, and turn us now;
Thou who hear'st Thy people's prayer,
End this dire intestine war.

Sprinkling us with Thy own blood,
Reconcile us first with God,
Then let all the British race
Kindly, cordially embrace.

Concord, on a distant shore,
To our countrymen restore;
Every obstacle remove,
Melt our hatred into love.

Gospel-grace to each extend,
Every foe, and every friend,
Then in Thee we sweetly find,
Peace with God and all mankind.[8]

The above lines, written seven years after the final paragraph of John Wesley's sermon at St. Matthew's, nevertheless provide an effective, rhythmic chorus to that address. The two passages illustrate once more how the work of the two brothers, especially their literary efforts, complemented each other.

The "Appeals"

Fairly early in the development of British Methodism, John Wesley had to rise in defense of his version of primitive religion, of the new evangelicalism. He had to prove, especially to the Anglican establishment, that Methodists in particular sought to strengthen, not to destroy, reason and order. Between 1743 and 1745, therefore, he puslished his "Appeals": *An Earnest Appeal to Men of Reason and Religion, A Farther Appeal to Men of Reason and Religion,* and the second and third parts of *A Farther Appeal.* The degree to which Wesley concerned himself to justify Methodism to the traditional religious institutions within eighteenth-century Britain may be understood through an awareness of the number of editions of the "Appeals" prepared by him during his lifetime. The *Earnest Appeal* went through ten editions between 1743 and 1786; the *Farther*

Appeal, Part I, five editions between 1745 and 1786; and Parts II and III of the *Farther Appeal* saw seven editions between 1745 and 1786.

Relatively early in the *Earnest Appeal,* in the twelfth paragraph, Wesley announced "That this is a short, rude sketch of the doctrine we teach. These are our fundamental principles; and we spend our lives in confirming others herein, and in a behaviour suitable to them."[9] The sketch develops into an argument of substance because Wesley, through his usual method, relies upon both Old and New Testaments. Just how much he does so is evident from a few statistics: of the 216 direct quotations in the *Earnest Appeal,* 184 (or 85 percent) are from the Bible—139 from the New Testament, 43 from the Old Testament, and 2 from the Apocrypha. Simply, the Methodist leader wanted every one of his opponents to realize the exact sources from which he derived the authority for his claims and the energy for his prose style.

Typical illustrations from *An Earnest Appeal,* those most likely to underscore Wesley's thesis and method, lie somewhere between those paragraphs heavily laden with direct quotations and the passages containing nothing beyond the writer's reactions and opinions. We may consider, first, the fifty-sixth paragraph, a part of the section wherein Wesley sets out to defend the doctrines that Methodists aspire to teach to others: secession from sin, salvation through faith, and perfection through Christian obedience. Thus—

> Now is it possible for any who believe the Scripture to deny one tittle of this? You can not. You dare not. You would not for the world. You know it is the pure Word of God. And this is the whole of what we preach. This is the height and depth of what we (with St. Paul) call perfection—a state of soul devoutly to be wished for by all who have tasted of the love of God. O pray for it without ceasing. It is the one thing you want. "Come with boldness to the throne of grace," and be assured that when you ask this of God you shall have "the petition you ask of him." We know indeed that "to man"—to the natural man—"this is impossible." But we know also that as "no work is impossible with God," so "all things are possible to him that believeth." (67)

Wesley's method is, indeed, structured upon clarity and simplicity; his manner, his tone, combines the staccato burst of the orator, of the field preacher, with the intellectual exercises of the learned scholar or the philosopher. The question thrusts itself forward; the answer comes back almost immediately, pounded out at least four times with the steady beat of the smith's hammer: "You can not. You dare not. You would not. . . . You know. . . ." Then, *almost exactly* half way through the paragraph,[10] the writer hurls upon the field the shield of Scriptures to substantiate—to display, as it were—the need for man to attain perfection. Wesley begins with a paraphrase of 1 Thessalonians 5:17 ("O . . . ceasing"), and then he weaves four quotations (Hebrews 4:16, 1 Samuel 1:27, Matthew 19:26, and Luke 1:37) into his sentence patterns to reach the conclusion of the final direct quotation—"all things are possible to him that believeth" (Mark 9:23).

The second *typical* example of Wesley's method of giving substance to his argument, the seventy-sixth paragraph, resembles the first in terms of length and the number of direct quotations;[11] yet, it presents a distinctly different emphasis:

You yourself can easily acquit us of this [of being Papists], but not of the other part of this charge. You still think we are secretly undermining, if not openly destroying, the Church. What do you mean by the Church? A visible Church (as our Article defines it) is "a company of faithful (or believing) people; *coetus credentium.*" This is the essence of a Church, and the properties thereof are (as they are described in the words that follow), "that the pure word of God be preached therein, and the sacraments duly administered." Now, then, according to this authentic account, what is the Church of England? What is it, indeed, but the *faithful people,* the *true believers* of England? It is true, if these are scattered abroad they come under another consideration. But when they are visibly joined by assembling together to hear "the pure word of God preached" and to "eat of one bread" and "drink of one cup," they are then properly "the visible Church of England."   (77)

Wesley, in the above passage, remains the preacher-scholar, this time striving hard to counter the accusation (one that would follow him for the remainder of his life) of Methodists being Papists. At the same time, however, he attempts to reach a workable definition of *Church.* Again, as in the first example, he relies upon a clear, succinct question as the focal point for the passage: "What do you mean by Church?" Again, as in the first example, Scripture provides the substance (although, in this instance, not the sound) for the answers, which turn out to be responses somewhat akin to congregational responsive readings. In this second example, however, Wesley, for obvious reasons, relies upon an institutional interpretation of Scripture rather than Scripture itself. Further, the direct quotations from *Ecclesiae Anglicanae* appear more evenly spaced throughout the passage, as opposed to the positioning of the five scriptural quotations in paragraph 56. Nevertheless, Wesley continues the practice of constructing the paragraph so that its conclusion comes to rest on a very concrete piece of evidence, in this case "the visible Church of England." The definition, at least in his own mind and for his own purpose, achieves an unquestionable and authoritative sense of completeness.[12]

Simple arithmetic tells us immediately that the *Earnest Appeal* did not put an end to John Wesley's need to declare his principles and his practices, as well as to defend his teachings. The length of the 1743 tract stands at approximately 19,500 words; the *Farther Appeal* contains some 91,400 words—40,500 in Part I, 28,500 in Part II, and 22,400 in Part III. Not only did Wesley feel the need to substantiate his arguments with careful attention to the images and language of Scriptures, he also undertook the responsibility for responding in considerable detail to specific writers who attacked both him and Methodism, as well as to analyze, with no less care, their works. His method, in that regard, was to deal lightly with little-known and even anonymous opponents, such as two tracts printed at Newcastle, *The Notions of the Methodists Fully Disproved* (24 pp.) and *The Notions of the Methodists Farther Disproved,* published separately in 1743 and then issued the following year in a single volume. However, if the attacker happened to be someone of rank and status within the Anglican establishment, then Wesley responded with considerable care and space. Thus, he replies to *Observations upon the Conduct of a Certain Sect usually distinguished by the Name of Methodists,* by Edmund Gibson, Bishop of Lincoln and London; to *A Charge delivered to the Reverend Clergy in the several parts of the Diocese of Lichfield and Coventry,* by Richard Smalbroke, Bishop of Lichfield and Coventry; and to a *Letter,* a general "cover preface" to Gibson's tract, by Thomas Herring, Archbishop of York and later of Canterbury. "Know ye not," Wesley asks these officers of his Church, "that the sound is gone forth into all the land? . . . That this religious concern has spread to every age and sex, to most orders and degrees of men?" (276).

Despite the length of the *Farther Appeal to Men of Reason,* the plan of each part is relatively simple. In Part I, he maintains that the doctrines of Methodism focus upon and indeed are derived from "the great truths of the gospel" (201). Thus faith remains, for the Methodist leader, the only means to salvation; without faith, there can be no such state as deliverance from sin and restoration of the soul. "The Author of faith and salvation is God alone," claims Wesley. "It is he that works in us both to will and to do. He is the sole giver of every good gift, and the sole author of every good work" (107). The second part considers the notion that although England refers to itself as a Christian nation, it has lost the concept of its Christian heritage. Wesley devotes much labor to the issue of the Old Testament Hebrews who neglected the ordinances of God, and then he chastises eighteenth-century Britons for looking aghast at such disobedience. He asks,

. . . how many thousands are found among us who have never partook of the Supper of the Lord? How many thousands are there that live and die in this unrepented obedience? What multitudes, even in this Christian city, do not attend any public worship at all? No, nor spend a single hour from one year to another in privately pouring out their hearts before God? (216)

The second part not only rebukes the members of the Church of England, but also points an accusing finger at Presbyterians, Independents, Baptists, Quakers, and Roman Catholics as foresakers of their respective traditions.

We need to keep in mind that the *Farther Appeal* directs itself to men of *reason* and religion, or to men whose religion comes from reason. Wesley maintains that Methodism is *"rational* as well as scriptural; it is as pure from enthusiasm as from superstition" (277). Therefore, in Part III, he advances the conclusion that *reasonable* men have no right or authority to attack Methodism; only *unreasonable* and *complacent* churchmen, rather than take action themselves to meet the needs of the people, simply sit back and accuse those who *do* react as empty enthusiasts. "O why," he pleads, "will you sink . . . poor souls deeper into perdition than they are sunk already? Why will you prophesy unto them peace, peace; when there is no peace? Why, if you do it not yourself (whether you cannot, or will not, God knoweth) should you hinder us from 'guiding them into the way of peace?' " (314).[13] Given the historical context in which that last part was written—the Jacobite uprising of 1745—

we can readily understand Wesley's concern about the apathy of the Church, its seeming refusal to comfort the people, to ease their fears. The Methodists, he asserts, provide and extend that comfort to all people, which in itself has created a "reformation of mankind" throughout the land. "By *reformation,* I mean, the bringing them back (not to this or that system of opinions or to this or that set of rites and ceremonies, how decent and significant soever; but) to the calm love of God and one another; to an uniform practice of justice, mercy, and truth" (322). Wesley thus summarizes the purpose and the function of his then young movement within the framework of the entire evangelical revival.

The Doctrine of Original Sin

In 1738, John Taylor, minister and schoolmaster at Kirkstead, Lincolnshire, published a tract entitled *The Scripture Doctrine of Original Sin proposed to Free and Candid Examination.*[14] The work came about as a result of Taylor's reaction to the harshness of the Calvinists' belief in original sin and their argument against the freedom of the will. The Calvinists maintained that people enter the world in a condition totally depraved, unable to do good or to avoid evil, unless directed by God. Sin, as explicated in Pauline teaching, entered the world through Adam. Because of him, many died, and his guilt carried over to his descendants—to all humanity. According to Taylor, however, sin existed as a purely personal matter. Certainly, he admitted that Adam's sin brought sorrow, labor, and physical death upon human beings, but that did not necessarily or automatically make them guilty or even corrupt them. In other words, although we *may* and actually *do* suffer because of Adam's sin (or Eve's sin), we cannot be punished for it, since we are not guilty of it. As human beings, we are not naturally inclined toward sin. Such humanitarian attitudes promote the ideas that corruption and moral sin are not universally present, that good predominates, and that virtue is latent in natural man. Such attitudes also brought two long-term results: (1) Taylor's essay proved instrumental, perhaps more than any work of its kind, in uprooting the traditions of Calvinism, both in England and in America; (2) it proved to be a fundamental document in preparing the way for the Unitarian movement in American Congregationalism.

Taylor's *Doctrine* stirred a veritable hornet's nest of indignation among American divines—at least eight responses (for and against) between 1757 and 1760, the last being the final work of Jonathan Edwards.[15] Across the ocean, however, reaction was limited. In 1740, Isaac Watts, whose hymns exhibited some inclination toward Calvinism, rose up to challenge Taylor in *The Ruin and Recovery of Mankind;* the 1767 edition of the *Doctrine* contained Taylor's reply. In 1757, John Wesley added to the debate by publishing his *The Doctrine of Original Sin, According to Scripture, Reason, and Experience.* Although Wesley, on 9 December 1758, complained to the seventeen-year-old Augustus Montague Toplady, then at Trinity College, Cambridge, that "no single person since Mahomet has given such a wound to Christianity as Dr. Taylor,"[16] the differences between the two never lowered one's respect for the other. "I esteem you as a person of uncommon sense and learning," wrote John Wesley to John Taylor on 3 July 1759, "but your doctrine I cannot esteem. . . ." Further, "it is certain, between you and me there need be no personal controversy at all; for we may agree to leave each other's person and character absolutely untouched, while we sum up and answer the several arguments advanced as plainly and closely as we can."[17] Although Taylor did not respond immediately, there appeared, after his death, an essay entitled *A Reply to the Rev. John Wesley's Remarks on the Scripture Doctrine of Original Sin.*

Wesley's *Doctrine* is an exceedingly lengthy tome of 270 pages and approximately 122,000 words. From his journals, we learn that Wesley began the project over six years prior to its publication; at Shackerley, near Manchester, on 10 April 1751, he noted, "Being now in the very midst of Mr. Taylor's disciples, I enlarged much more than I am accustomed to do on the doctrine of Original Sin; and determined, if God should give me a few years' life, publicly to answer his new gospel."[18] In his preface, written from Lewisham and dated 30 November 1756, he credits Taylor as "a person of sense, nay of unusually strong understanding, joined with no small liveliness of imagination, and a good degree of various learning." Nevertheless, the author of the 1738 tract is presented as a theological confidence man, the author of a "scheme . . . far more dangerous than open Deism itself. It does not shock us like barefaced infidelity: We feel no pain, and suspect no evil, while it [his *Doctrine*] steals 'like water into our bowels,' like 'oil into our bones'." It all leads, for John Wesley, to nothing but the "old Deism in a new dress; seeing it saps the foundation of all revealed religion, whether Jewish or Christian."[19]

Theologically, Wesley was an Arminian,[20] which meant that he adhered to the idea of Divine sovereignty being compatible with a real free will in all human beings. Christ died for *all*, not only for the elect; thus, predestination was unbiblical. He came into conflict with Taylor not as a result of the latter's opposition to Calvinism, but because he considered Taylor's arguments as destructive of evangelicalism; simply, they did not sufficiently recognize God's grace in the overall ideal of human regeneration. In addition, Wesley became deeply irritated because, he thought, Taylor relied too heavily upon Scriptures to support his doctrines. Wesley therefore devotes a large segment of each section of his work to detailed analyses of various texts, both in support of and in opposition to Taylor's doctrine. Often he strays so far off the mark, or becomes so involved, that he seems to lose his readers as well as himself. Nonetheless, he always manages to find his way back home again:

The preceding texts were brought to prove (and they do so abundantly prove it) that our nature is deeply corrupted, inclined to evil, and disinclined to all that is spiritually good; so that, without supernatural grace, we can neither will nor do what is pleasing to God. And this easily accounts for the wickedness and misery of mankind in all ages and nations; whereby experience and reason do so strongly confirm this scriptural doctrine of original sin.   (273)

Because of the extent to which Wesley piles quotation upon quotation and reference upon reference, to analyze and to explicate his *Doctrine of Original Sin* becomes no easy task. In fact, we really need to ask ourselves, on more than one occasion, whether we should give Wesley credit for writing or for compiling this tract. Still, he does manage to stamp upon its pages his mark as an organizer, his ability to control for the most part large quantities of complex and diverse material and to parade them in orderly fashion before his readers. Thus, in Part I, he conducts a survey of man in all ages and in all countries. Part II consists of a defense of the doctrine of original sin through what Wesley labels "the Scriptural method," while the third section addresses Taylor's Supplement, wherein the Presbyterian divine responded to Isaac Watts's *Ruin and Recovery of Mankind* and to *A Vindication of the Scripture Doctrine of Original Sin* by the respected Dissenter of Gravel Lane, Wapping, David Jennings. Wesley dissects and refutes each one of the eight sections of the

Supplement. Part IV contains extracts from Watts's essay, and in Part V Wesley abstracts a tract by an obscure cleric who also wrote in opposition to John Taylor: Samuel Hebden, minister of Wrentham, Suffolk, and author of *The Ruin and Recovery of Human Nature*. In Part VI, he returns to the subject at hand and supplies still another abstract, this one of Jennings's *Vindication*.

Wesley brings his encyclopedia on original sin to a conclusion with Part VII, an abstract (not surprisingly) of a longtime popular classic of Calvinistic theology, *Human Nature in Its Fourfold State*, by Thomas Boston the elder. Wesley really believed that Boston provided the anti-Taylorites with the necessary "legal" force with which to hold their readers to the traditional doctrines:

Adam, by his sin, became not only guilty, but corrupt; and so transmits guilt and corruption to his posterity. By this sin he stripped himself of his original righteousness and corrupted himself. We were in him representatively, as our moral head; we were in him seminally, as our natural head. Hence we fell in him; (as Levi "paid tithes" when "in the loins of Abraham;") "by his disobedience" we "were made sinners;" his first sin is imputed to us. (458)

However, it is John Wesley who has the final word, who provides the *emotive* force against John Taylor by appealing directly to the author of *Scriptural Doctrine of Original Sin:* "O Sir," begs the leader of the Methodists, "think it possible that you may have been mistaken! that you may have leaned too far, for what you thought the better extreme! Be persuaded once more to review your whole cause, and that from the very foundation. And in doing so, you will not disdain to desire more than natural light" (433). Strangely enough, Wesley formed the opinion that Taylor actually did *review his whole cause*. Writing to Sir Harry Trelawney in August 1780, he admitted to having "reason, indeed, to believe he [Taylor] was convinced of his mistake some years before he died. But to acknowledge this publicly was too hard a task for one who had lived above eighty years."[21]

Plain Account of Christian Perfection

Wesley, who responded quickly to certain controversies generated by others, was certainly not above developing and advancing his own controversial doctrines. Midway through the maturation period of British Methodism, he publicized his stand on *perfection,* which, traditionally and absolutely, had been attributed only to God.

Wesley, taking his cue first from Matthew 5:48—"Be ye therefore perfect, even as your Father which is in Heaven is perfect"—and from William Law's *Practical Treatise on Christian Perfection* (1726), determined perfection to be an instantaneous experience that occurs sometime after conversion, convincing those who receive it that sin can be rooted out from them. In addition, he intended the term *Christian perfection* to mean "the humble, gentle, patient love of God, and our neighbour, ruling our tempers, words, and actions."[22] To explain and defend his doctrine, he published *A Plain Account of Christian Perfection, As Believed and Taught by the Rev. Mr. John Wesley, from the Year 1725 to the Year 1765,* a book of 162 pages that he saw fit to revise on several occasions.[23]

"What I propose," wrote Wesley in the opening paragraph, ". . . is, to give a plain and distinct account of the steps by which I was led, during a course of many years, to embrace the doctrine of Christian perfection" (366). He then displays for the reader the works that shaped his decisions and directed him toward the doctrine of perfection; for those of us already exposed to the education of John Wesley, these are familiar volumes: Taylor's *Holy Living* and *Holy Dying, The Christian Pattern* of Thomas à Kempis, Law's *Christian Perfection* and *Serious Call.* The mention of and slight discussion about those tracts set the tone for the entire volume; Wesley intends only to go over old territory, to synthesize views that he has held for over forty years. In fact, by the end of the volume, in the next to the last paragraph, he has come full circle: "I have now done what I proposed. I have given a plain and simple account of the manner wherein I first received the doctrine of perfection, and the sense wherein I received, and wherein I do receive, and teach it to this day" (443). The tract comes to an end with a series of inquiries into the reasons for all of the controversy over Christian perfection when no valid reasons for or real substance to such outcries and arguments really exist. "Why," asks Wesley (not really expecting or even wanting a reply), "should devout men be afraid of devoting all their soul, body, and substance to God? Why should those who love Christ count it a damnable error, to think we may have all the mind that was in him?" (445).

Even though the *Plain Account of Christian Perfection* offered its readers little more than a review of what most of them probably

already knew, the volume seems worthy of discussion, particularly
for those who remain attentive to John Wesley's prose style and
rhetorical techniques. What immediately catches the eye is the
number of poetic illustrations to support the explanation and defense
of the doctrine of perfection: twenty-one pieces of poetry, ranging
in length from a single stanza to a complete poem of nine stanzas,
all of which were written by Charles or John Wesley. In quoting
from his and his brother's earliest poetic efforts (1736, 1738, 1739),
Wesley announces to his detractors that his sentiments concerning
perfection were formed early, became public for all to observe, and,
for all purposes, have not changed radically. Thus, from *Hymns and
Sacred Poems* (1739), he reproduces this declaration:

> Eager for thee I ask and pant,
> So strong the principle divine,
> Carries me out with sweet constraint,
> Till all my hallow'd soul be thine;
> Plunged in the Godhead's deepest sea,
> And lost in thine immensity!
> (370)

Wesley really believes that the example from the poetry cannot be
challenged seriously by reasonable men. In one instance, he states
that "It would be easy to cite many more passages to the same effect.
But these are sufficient to show, beyond contradiction, what our
sentiments then were" (370). "Can anything be more clear . . . ?"
he asks (382) after citing a hymn from a 1741 poetic collection.
Finally, portions of three hymns from the 1742 volume of the
brothers' poems demonstrate that "there is no contrariety at all
between our first and our last sentiments"; the intention has already
been, and will continue, to "Enter into thy promised rest; / The.
Canaan of thy perfect love!" (385, 386).

If poetry cannot sway the doubters, then Wesley rushes into the
breach extracts from the minutes of Methodist annual conferences
to demonstrate that Christian perfection has existed as a regular
agenda item since the beginning of the first conference in June
1744. The proceedings of those gatherings went forward, principally, upon the format of question and answer, especially on matters
concerning doctrine. And, since Wesley supplied all of the answers,
the general tone of the minutes is one of authority; Wesley's response

provided the answer to the question, or the solution to the problem, and eliminated, as far as he was concerned, the need for further discussion. Asked whether those who have attained perfection still require Christ, Wesley replies,

> In every state we need Christ in the following respects. (1) Whatever grace we receive, it is a free gift from him. (2) We receive it as his purchase, merely in consideration of the price he paid. (3) We have this grace, not only from Christ, but in him. For our perfection is not like that of a tree, which flourishes by the sap derived from its own root, but, as was said before, like that of a branch which, united to the vine, bears fruit; but, severed from it, is dried up and withered. (4) All our blessings, temporal, spiritual, and eternal, depend on his intercession for us, which is one branch of his priestly office, whereof therefore we have always equal need. (5) The best of men still need Christ in his priestly office, to atone for their omissions, their short-comings, (as some not improperly speak,) their mistakes in judgment and practice, and their defects of various kinds.
>
> (395–96)

As with the poetry quotation, the extracts from the conference minutes attempt to provide substance to Wesley's doctrine, consistency to his defense of the doctrine, and authority to his position as leader of the movement that advanced the doctrine. Throughout his *Christian Perfection,* he never varies from his position that perfection, though not absolute, does indeed exist, and that those who have attained it "never before, had so deep, so unspeakable, a conviction of the need of Christ in all his offices as they have now" (443).

Chapter Six
Biographical and Critical Prose

When John Wesley entered a religious or political debate, he did so from a position of strength. His simple, terse, direct style; his calm, reasonable tone; his intense, penetrating sincerity: all of those qualities carried the day against the impassioned harangues, the invective and vituperation, of his attackers. His prose style, moreover, reflected his character; he emerged from the printed page as the scholar and the gentleman, the priestly don—sometimes oversimplistic, sometimes repetitive, but always neat, gentle, and pious.

But when left to generate ideas of his own rather than respond to the ideas of others, Wesley failed to produce much prose that can be termed original or even forceful. He may have been one of eighteenth-century England's great men in terms of purpose and action, but he was not one of eighteenth-century England's great thinkers. Wesley's problem centered on his almost total reliance upon the Bible as a means for arriving at intellectual decisions. He embraced every word from that book, and when it came time to consider the themes, the ideas, and the efforts of his contemporaries, he filtered practically every phrase through his honest but nevertheless restrictive system of scriptural proof. Thus he ran the risk of seriously negating, both for himself and for his followers, a number of noteworthy historical, philosophical, and even ethical issues of his own times. In a word, John Wesley's critical awareness was so strongly impaired by his theological views that he tended to turn his back upon certain writers for reasons that seemed not always to be clear or even sound.

Consider these instances. John Wesley evidenced absolutely no patience with unorthodox approaches to biblical commentary. "It would be excusable," he wrote, "if these menders of the Bible would offer their hypotheses modestly. But one cannot excuse them when they not only obtrude their novel scheme with the utmost confidence, but even ridicule that scriptural one which always was, and is now, held by men of the greatest learning and piety in the world. Hereby they promote the cause of infidelity more effectually than either Hume or Voltaire."[1] Thus he is quite pleased after reading James Beattie's *Essay on the Nature and Immutability of Truth in Opposition to Sophistry and Superstition*. Beattie, maintains Wesley, is more than a match for Hume, "the most insolent despiser of truth and virtue that ever appeared in the world . . . an avowed enemy to God and man and to all that is sacred and valuable upon earth."[2] Finally, he condemns Sir John Dalrymple for his *Memoirs of Great Britain and Ireland, from the Dissolution of the Last Parliament of Charles II, until the Sea Battle off La Hogue*, observing that "He believes just as much of the Bible as David Hume did. Hence he perpetually ascribes to enthusiasm whatever good men did from a strong conviction of duty."[3] What Wesley failed to understand about Hume was that the Scottish philosopher concerned himself principally with satisfying his own curiosity; unlike Wesley, he cared little for seeking out and then supplying additional lumber for the defense of biblical authority.

More than sixty years after its occurrence, Wesley chose to react to the controversy between Samuel Clarke, rector of St. James's, Westminster, and the German philosopher and mathematician Gottfried Wilhelm Leibnitz, who advanced the idea of matter as a multitude of *monads*, each a nucleus of force and a microcosm or concentration of the universe. Admitting that the interaction of spirit is inexplicable, Leibnitz assumed a preestablished harmony between them. Further, he maintained the spirit to be modified by final causes, while bodies were modified by efficient causes. The two series came together, somewhat like two clocks striking in unison, by a harmony established for all time by God, the supreme *monad* and perfect exemplar of the human soul. Leibnitz explicated his theory first in a popular piece entitled *Theodicee*, published in 1710; he expanded upon it in a more serious vein four years later, in *Monadologie*. Clarke's opposition took the form of correspondence with Leibnitz, entitled *A Collection of Papers . . . relating to the Principles of Natural Philosophy and Religion*, wherein he dealt with time and space and their relations to God and moral freedom.

On 14 September 1770, in a letter to Richard Locke, surveyor of Burnham parish, near Bristol, concerning proper reading habits,

Wesley advised the avoidance of Leibnitz, who "would only unhinge and perplex your mind."[4] Almost five years later, he is more emphatic and certainly more specific about the philosopher. In his journal for 22 May 1775, Wesley asks,

And is this he whom the King of Prussia extols, as something more than human? So poor a writer have I seldom read, either as to sentiments or temper. In sentiment he is a thorough fatalist, maintaining roundly, and without reserve, that God has absolutely decreed from all eternity whatever is done in time; and that no creature can do more good, or less evil, than God has pre-emptorily decreed. And his temper is just suitable to his sentiments. He is haughty, self-conceited, sour, impatient of contradiction, and holds his opponent[5] in utter contempt; though, in truth, he is but a child in his hands.[6]

In Wesley's defense, we must remember that he was raised and educated during a period (roughly 1700 to 1740) of intense religious controversy; attacks upon orthodox doctrines appeared regularly, and almost all of those were answered with the same degree of speed and frequency. Wesley's reaction to Leibnitz, then, is instinctive— a form of intellectual reflex action that he chose to record in his journals.

Nonetheless, we cannot excuse Wesley when his prejudices run so deeply that they dull his critical acumen to the point where he casts negative shadows upon that which he generally considered acceptable and worthwhile. For example, Wesley admits to being "delighted" by the first part of Thomas Reid's 1764 *Inquiry into the Human Mind*, but "disappointed" by the remainder. Why? "I doubt whether the sentiments are just; but I am sure his language is so obscure that to most readers it must be mere Arabic."[7] But Wesley is not really concerned with Reid's style; rather, he attacks the Scottish philosopher because he praises "that prodigy of self-conceit, Rousseau—a shallow but supercillious infidel, two degrees below Voltaire! Is it possible that a man who admires him can admire the Bible?" (*Journal*, 6:23). Because Rousseau and Voltaire rank so high on Wesley's list of arch-fiends, he simply cannot, in the light of reason, undertake a clear discussion of any work in which the writer inclines toward a positive attitude about one, the other, or both. Similar examples abound throughout Wesley's critical prose.

A similar problem arises on the occasion of Wesley's reaction to the 1777 *History of America*, written by the eminent Scottish historian William Robertson. Despite Robertson's achievements in his *History of Scotland* and *History of Charles V*—Wesley read both and especially admired the former—the Methodist leader finds the inevitable flaw. "I cannot admire," he asserts, ". . . a Christian divine writing a history with so little of Christianity in it. Nay, he seems studiously to avoid anything which might imply that he believes in the Bible."[8] Wesley has not finished with Robertson, however, for he has committed a sin equal to that of his countryman Thomas Reid. He has demonstrated an affinity for another on the list of Wesley's arch-infidels, Henry Home, Lord Kames, the Scot jurist and critic who wrote (among other titles) a two-volume *Sketches of the History of Man* (1774), a piece that Wesley particularly disliked. Thus Wesley leaps at Robertson's throat for "his speaking so honourably of a professed infidel; yea, and referring to his masterpiece of infidelity, *Sketches of the History of Man*, as artful, as unfair, as disingenuous a book as even Toland's *Nazarenus*."[9] But Wesley is not yet finished with Robertson; he accuses the historian of "copying after Dr. Hawkesworth[10] . . . in totally excluding the Creator from governing the world. Was it not enough, never to mention the providence of God, where there was the fairest occasion, without saying expressly, 'The *fortune of Certiz*,' or '*chance*,' did thus or thus? So far as fortune or chance governs the world, God has no place in it."[11]

The above are but four examples of Wesley's reactions to writers of note who simply failed to embrace or to give proper emphasis to his forms of orthodoxy. We could easily expand the discussion to include his attacks upon Sterne, Smollett, Swedenborg, drama, the novel, and a host of contemporary persons, issues, and forms with which the leader of Methodism could not bring himself to reach a compromise. And, perhaps even unconsciously, that inability to compromise finds its way into his biographical works and literary criticism. Thus we may often observe instances when Wesley attacks and defends writers and their works on grounds that appear highly artificial or, at best, unnecessary. Yet, even in those seemingly shallow contexts, he never lost sight of the need to *educate* his readers, to mold them into "thinking" Christians whose minds and spirits would be elevated by what they read, and whose orthodoxy would be strengthened by reading what he told them to read and discarding what he told them to cast aside. Unfortunately, the value of John

Wesley's stock diminishes when he becomes the guardian of his followers' intellects, as well as of their morals.

Life of John Fletcher

John William Fletcher (originally *de la Flechere*), a native of Nyon, Switzerland, came to England in 1752 from the Swiss military, then in service to the King of Portugal, and obtained a tutorship in the family of Thomas Hill, M.P., at Tern Hall, Shropshire. At the time of the parliamentary session, he accompanied the family to London, came in contact with the Wesleyan Methodists, and promptly joined the society at West Street. Wesley encouraged Fletcher to take orders; thus, in 1757, he was ordained at Whitehall, after which he rushed off to assist Wesley, with whom he remained in close association until his death. In 1760, he was appointed vicar of Madeley, some ten miles from Tern Hall; ten years later, Selina Shirley, Countess of Huntingdon and the patroness of George Whitefield and the Calvinist Methodists, appointed Fletcher head of her seminary at Trevecca, in Wales. He served there for only one year, his departure necessitated by the countess's purge of Wesleyan Methodists from her institution. From Wales he returned to London, to Switzerland, back to Madeley, then, because of ill health, to the hot wells outside Bristol. In November 1781, he wed Mary Bosanquet, one of John Wesley's most devoted female workers, and the couple settled in Madeley. Throughout adulthood, Fletcher suffered from consumption; his death in mid-August 1785 was a severe blow to the aged Wesley, who preached his funeral sermon on 6 November. By early August 1786, the Methodist patriarch was at work on Fletcher's biography; the preface, written at Amsterdam, is dated 12 September 1786, and the work appeared in published form in December under the title *A Short Account of the Life and Death of the Reverend John Fletcher.*

Inevitably, concerning the period 1660–1789, there arises the temptation to undertake a pilgrimage to eighteenth-century England's biographical shrine for the purpose of comparing a particular biography with the *Life of Johnson*. To yield to such temptation is a serious mistake, since few of Boswell's contemporaries possessed his abilities to make biography an art: to filter fact and reaction to fact through the imagination without sacrificing factual accuracy, to develop the character of his subject as well as to explicate his words and his literary activities. And, of course, few of Boswell's contemporaries found subjects as complete and as dimensional as Samuel Johnson; few eighteenth-century biographers were able to make contact with a subject whose ideas and reactions would allow room for dramatic interpretation. In the end, both Boswell *and* Johnson—both biographer *and* subject—shared the responsibility and the credit for producing a work that has become nothing less than a classic work of literature, an example of artistic achievement.

At age eighty-three, John Wesley had neither the time nor the energy to attempt artistic achievement. True, he had known his subject for almost thirty-five years, and certainly his relationship with John Fletcher appeared more filial than purely personal or professional. Wesley viewed his biographical project, however, as one more of his countless responsibilities brought on by the necessity to report, as quickly as possible, the life and work of a dedicated individual and to distribute his account, with equal expedition, among his followers, identifying Fletcher as a model Christian whom all Methodists would do well to emulate. In that context, he entitled his biography *A Short Account*, noting in his preface that "I . . . think myself obliged by the strongest ties to pay this small tribute to his memory."[12] Therefore, we can understand the apparent contradiction that Wesley himself calls to our attention. From the outset he indicates that his relationship with John Fletcher was no "slight or ordinary acquaintance; but we were of one heart and of one soul. We had no secrets between us for many years; we did not purposely hide anything from each other. From time to time he consulted me, and I him, on the most important occasions; and he constantly professed, not only much esteem, but, what I valued far more, much affection" (275). Nevertheless, in the very next paragraph, Wesley tells us that we will not see the biographical fruits of this extraordinary acquaintance; we will not be too much a part of those important occasions during which pupil and master, biographer and subject, consulted with each other. Instead, we are to "observe, that . . . I am little more than a compiler; for I owe a great, if not the greatest, part of the ensuing Tract to a few friends, who have been at no small pains in furnishing me with materials; and above all, to my dear friend, (such as she has been almost from her childhood,) Mrs. Fletcher" (275–76).

We have indicated on more than one occasion throughout these discussions of John Wesley's prose that the leader of the Methodists possessed the ability, which he developed while a tutor at Lincoln College, Oxford, to extract, arrange, and assemble a considerable quantity and variety of material from the works of other writers and to recast it for his own purposes. In other words, during the more than fifty years during which he put pen to paper, he demonstrated far greater skill as an editor than as a writer. From another point of view, he found more opportunities to edit than to write; because he was pressed by the demands of his responsibilities, time did not permit the luxury of creativity, but merely allowed for quick compilation. It thus comes as no surprise to discover that, of the approximately 45,000 words in the *Life and Death of Fletcher*, less than 10 percent was actually *written* by John Wesley; the remainder of the work is comprised of fifty-two separate narratives from seventeen sources—including twenty of Fletcher's letters to various persons, six personal accounts by Mary Fletcher, and five accounts supplied by a Mr. Vaughan, a servant of Thomas Hill at Tern Hall.

Wesley's method, then, is generally to provide a broad introduction to a chapter, and then to turn it over to one or more of the sources. For instance, in Chapter IV, "From His Settling at Madeley, to His Leaving Trevecka," Wesley's main purpose focuses upon explaining Fletcher's position at Trevecca College in relation to the controversy then existing between the Wesleyan Methodists and the Countess of Huntingdon's connection. He believes it "my bounden duty to clear up the whole affair. And I cannot do this better than by transcribing the substance of an account which I have received from Mr. Benson,[13] in answer to my inquiries" (293–94). Then follow twelve paragraphs of Benson's account, interrupted only by the insertion of three letters written by Fletcher, the last of which concludes the chapter. In Chapter VI, "From His Leaving Newington, till His Return from Switzerland to Madeley," we may observe a variation on the above method: Wesley supplies the opening two sentences, then hands the narrative over to a Miss Thornton, who carries on for two paragraphs. Then follow (1) three letters from Fletcher, (2) four paragraphs of Wesley's version of events, (3) another letter from Fletcher, (4) two letters from a Mr. Ireland, who accompanied Fletcher to France and Switzerland, (5) a transition paragraph by Wesley, (6) two letters from Fletcher, (7) a lengthy letter from William Perronet, (8) a one-paragraph comment upon Perronet's letter by Fletcher, (9) a second letter from William Perronet, (10) another letter by Fletcher, (11) an anecdotal paragraph by Wesley, (12) a paragraph of narration by Mr. Ireland, (13) another paragraph of narration by Wesley, and finally (14) four letters by Fletcher to conclude the chapter. Thus, the chapter contains sixty-one paragraphs: Wesley wrote but seven of those (11.5 percent) and included eleven of Fletcher's letters—more than half of the total number of his letters inserted into the entire biography.

Of course, the conditions of the moment really dictated Wesley's method in preparing his account of John Fletcher. Not only was he in a hurry to finish the work and get it out before the public, but he had to compensate for his difficulty in providing a complete and comprehensive account of Fletcher's life and character. Wesley explains, almost in a tone of complaint or exasperation:

> He was upon all occasions very uncommonly reserved in speaking of himself, whether in writing or conversation. He hardly ever said anything concerning himself, unless it slipped from him unawares. And among the great number of papers which he has left, there is scarce a page (except that single account of his conversion to God) relative either to his own inward experience, or the transactions of his life. So that the most of the information we have is gathered up, either from short hints scattered up and down in his letters, from what he had occasionally dropped among his friends, or from what one and another remembered concerning him.
> (340)

Then, in a display of modesty even too extreme for John Wesley, he admits to being "sensible of my own inability to draw such a portrait as Mr. Fletcher deserves. I have no turn at all for panegyric: I have never accustomed myself to it. It gives me therefore no small satisfaction to find, that this is in a great measure done to my hands. The picture is already drawn; and that by no mean pencil" (341). With that, he simply turns the matter of Fletcher's character over to Mary Fletcher, who—with the help of bits and pieces from others' narratives and some additional of her husband's letters—completes the chapter.

John Wesley's ability as a writer, as a biographer, is never really in question here. In fact, if his motive ("to pay small tribute to his memory") is clear, his purpose seems even clearer. Simply, he wished to *compile* (as he has told us) an account of John Fletcher's life and character, but he did not wish to inject himself into that account. Only an insensitive fool can read Boswell's *Life of Johnson* and be unaware of Boswell's presence; only the most discerning mind can read Wesley's *Life of Fletcher* and be aware of Wesley. Ever so skill-fully—as a most skillful editor—the leader of the Methodists loses himself within the events and the thoughts of Methodism's most prominent disciple, caring nothing about his own artistic achieve-ment and even less about his own literary reputation. In detaching himself from his subject, in burying himself amidst facts and ac-counts, narratives and letters, John Wesley fulfills his goal: he keeps his distance in order to pay tribute to one whom he loved dearly.

Thoughts on Prior

In 1782, Wesley published a seven-page essay, the title of which would lead readers to believe that he will discuss *Thoughts on the Character and Writings of Mr. Prior*. However, we need not proceed much beyond the first sentence before realizing that Wesley has no intention of developing a discussion on Matthew Prior's writing or his character. Instead, he proceeds to take issue with "A very in-genious writer [who] has lately given us a particular account of the character and Works of Mr. Prior."[14] The problem stems from the unidentified writer's reliance "on the testimony of very suspicious witnesses," namely Alexander Pope and Joseph Spence;[15] both, claims Wesley, "depreciated him [Prior] to exalt themselves" (480). Throughout the essay, Wesley never mentions the name of his "very ingenious writer"; nonetheless, the evidence points directly to Sam-uel Johnson and that writer's *Life of Prior*, which, in turn, permits Wesley's *Thoughts on Prior* to be placed among the so-called oppo-sition pieces to Johnson's *Lives of the Poets* published during the latter's lifetime. But because the essay has occupied an inconspicuous niche in Wesley's collected works, few (if indeed any!) students of either Wesley or Johnson have even bothered to identify the object of the Methodist leader's irritation as the sage of Bolt Court.

Certainly Wesley's reasons for responding to Johnson's critical comments arose not from any personal dislike for the London poet, scholar, lexicographer, philosopher, and critic. Instead, the essay probably had its origins in the esteem that at least three Wesleys—Samuel the younger, John, and Charles—held for Matthew Prior. Samuel Wesley the younger knew the poet during the period when the former served as usher at Westminster School and Bishop Francis Atterbury held the office of Dean of Westminster. Prior and the dean were close political allies; Wesley, as an equally close com-

panion of Atterbury, visited frequently with the poet. John's opportunity for contact with Prior came during his last years at
Charterhouse, when he visited his elder brother, while Charles's
association came only by reading Prior's work. Professor Henry Bett,
although unable to identify the author of the commentary on Prior's
verse to which Wesley reacts, can nevertheless cite sixteen examples
from the Wesleys' hymns, most of them authored by Charles, wherein
the influence of Matthew Prior is strongly evident.[16] However, the
Wesleys' view of Prior transcended simple matters of poetic influence
and imitation. Either firsthand or by way of the printed page, the
brothers discovered in this Augustan poet a model of perfection for
eighteenth-century man: the scholar, the poet, the statesman whose
Tory principles anchored him firmly to the trinity of God, king,
and nation, and whose sense of loyalty allowed him to endure harassment and even persecution from an overzealous Whig ministry.

The real attraction of Wesley's *Thoughts on Prior* is the Methodist
leader's handling of Johnson's ideas and language, especially in light
of his knowing the London critic and possessing considerable respect
for his person and reputation. In fact, what Wesley does with bits
and pieces from the *Life of Prior* is outright amazing! As stated
previously, the title of Johnson's essay and the name of Samuel
Johnson never appear; only on one occasion does Wesley let down
his guard:

> But it is said, "'Henry and Emma' is a dull and tedious dialogue, which
> excites neither esteem for the man, nor tenderness for the woman." Does
> it not? Then I know not with what eyes, or with what heart, a man must
> read it. "Dull and tedious!" See how Doctors differ! One who was no bad
> poet himself, and no bad judge of poetry . . . spoke of this very poem
> as one of the finest in the English language.   (421–22)

Otherwise, the only two names mentioned (other than that of Prior)
are Pope and Spence, and unsuspecting or unenlightened readers
may well be duped into believing that one or the other is the "very
ingenious writer." At one point, after providing what appears to
be a direct quotation from Spence relative to Prior's low moral state,
Wesley declares that "I am well assured, my eldest brother would
have had no acquaintance with him [Prior], had he been such a
wretch as Mr. Spence describes" (419). As for Pope, Wesley devotes
four of the last five paragraphs of his essay to an attack upon the

Elegy to the Memory of an Unfortunate Lady, conveying the impression that the author of such an irreligious piece ("Consummate nonsense!" he terms it) ought not to hurl negative criticism against Matthew Prior, whose "knowledge of religion and of the Scriptures [was] far greater" (424).

Between Spence and Pope lies an unrecognizable Johnsonian prose—or, at least, *attempts* to make Johnson's prose unrecognizable. Wesley offers his readers what appear to be eleven direct quotations from the *Life of Prior*, not one of which is presented accurately. Wesley's method is, simply, to cite a critical comment from the "ingenious writer" and then counter it with his own comments:

> But "his amorous effusions have neither gallantry nor tenderness. They are the dull exercises of one trying to be amorous by dint of study. When he tries to act the lover, his thoughts are unaffecting and remote. In his amorous pedantry he exhibits the College."   (421)

Now, notice the original in Johnson's *Life of Prior*:

> In *his Amorous Effusions* he is less happy; for they are not dedicated by nature or by passion, and *have neither gallantry nor tenderness*. *They* have the coldness of Cowley without his wit; *the dull exercises* of a skilful versifier resolved at all adventures to write something about Chloe, and *trying* to be amorous by dint of study. [17]

Wesley then omits the next *seventy-seven* words and picks up his version of the quotation in the *middle* of the next to last sentence of the original paragraph: ". . . *when he tries to act the lover* without the help of gods and goddesses *his thoughts are unaffecting or remote*" (202). The final sentence in Wesley's version of the quotation—"In his amorous pedantry he exhibits the College"—does not even appear in Johnson's *Life of Prior*!

Knowing Wesley as we do, his intention in the above "misquotation" is fairly clear. Essentially, he reverts to his old habits as an extractor or editor of another's words and thoughts, seemingly without any deep concern for the *exactness* of the original. At Lincoln College, he presented his students with Shakespeare, Milton, Donne, and Herbert according to his own sense of what they should or should not learn from those writers. He does the same with Samuel Johnson for his fellow Methodists. In his dealings with other writers,

Wesley, obviously taking his moral and intellectual guardianship with extreme seriousness, wields the heavy hand of moral censorship or, at least, turns the screws of intellectual slanting. In regard to the previous quotation on Prior's "amorous effusions," Wesley blots out the substance of Johnson's paragraph, specifically Prior's use of classical imagery. Once more the intention is clear, since any discussion of heathen deities (in this instance Venus, Cupid, Diana, Mercury, Jupiter) is alien to Wesley's "Christian tastes." In fact, he bases his entire defense of Prior on that poet's religious or moral verse, virtually ignoring everything else he had written.

We may consider another aspect of Wesley's restructuring of Johnson's sentences, that of negating (or, at least, having the effect of negating) the true artistry of Johnson's prose style. According to Wesley, the "ingenious writer" complains that "his [Prior's] numbers commonly want ease, airiness, lightness, and facility." Further, "but even what is smooth is not soft" (420). Now, let us observe carefully *exactly* what Wesley has omitted:

> *His numbers* are such as mere diligence may attain; they seldom offend the ear, and seldom sooth it; they *commonly want airiness, lightness and facility*; *what is smooth is not soft*. His verses always roll, but they seldom flow.   (210; my italics)

To appreciate Johnson's prose style, which is to appreciate his competence for judging the works of others with an eye toward balance, we must realize that he was seriously concerned with proportion. At times he leaned toward the negative, at times he inclined toward the positive, at times he achieved almost perfect neutrality (or balance); but he always created a sense of proportion. The paragraph quoted above concerning Prior's numbers contains *nine* items; on the positive side, Johnson concludes that Prior's meter

    1. seldom offends the ear
    2. contains some smoothness
    3. allows his verses to "roll"

From a negative view, however, the poet's "numbers"

    1. are products of mere diligence
    2. seldom soothe the ear

3. lack airiness
4. lack lightness
5. lack softness
6. hinder the flow of his verses

Wesley never allows his readers to come to grips with the details of Johnson's argument; instead, he sets down only those items with which he desires to take sharp issue. Why? So that in the end, he can filter Prior's poetic habits through his own moral screen of critical criteria: "In truth," writes Wesley, "the general fault of Prior's poetry is this: It is not too much, but too little laboured" (420).

The last of Wesley's rhetorical sins comes at the beginning of his *Thoughts*. At the outset of the second paragraph he states—and does so *without* quotation marks—"Mr. Pope gives it as his opinion, that he [Prior] was fit only to make verses. What can be more unjust?" (418). From one point of view, the question answers itself if we look at what appears in Johnson's *Life of Prior*: "He [Prior] was, however, in Pope's opinion fit only to make verses and less qualified for business than Addison himself. This was surely said without consideration" (198). Wesley is so eager to leap at Pope's throat that he conveniently loses sight of the thesis of Johnson's paragraph; the latter actually defends Matthew Prior against Pope's criticism, maintaining that Joseph Addison's political failures came about because of his own incompetence in carrying out the duties to which he was assigned. Prior, on the other hand, *succeeded* because he "was employed by men very capable of estimating his value," being "at last sent to transact a negotiation in the highest degree arduous and important . . ." (198).

For John Wesley, Johnson's *Life of Prior*—the London or Dublin edition of 1779, or the Dublin or London edition of 1781—provided an opportunity to discolor the poetic reputation of Pope and to elevate the moral and artistic statures of Matthew Prior. "Upon the whole," he declares at the end of his *Thoughts*, "I cannot but think that the natural understanding of Mr. Prior was far stronger than that of Mr. Pope; that his judgment was more correct, his learning more extensive. . . . And I conceive his poetic abilities were at least equal to those either of Pope or Dryden" (424). Such a statement shocks even the slow-witted among us, but we must recover quickly and remember that Wesley's critical criteria are *moral* criteria. For the founder and leader of British Methodism, the triumph of Matthew Prior over Alexander Pope is the moral and religious superiority of this passage—

> Yet, if he wills, may change or spoil the whole;
> May take yon beauteous, mystic, starry roll,
> And burn it, like an useless parchment scroll;
> May from its basis in one moment pour
> This melted earth
> Like liquid metal, and like burning ore;
> Who sole in power, at the beginning said,
> "Let sea, and air, and earth, and heaven be made,
> And it was so;" and when he shall ordain
> In other sort, has but to speak again,
> And they shall be no more: Of this great theme,
> This glorious, hallow'd, everlasting name,
> This God, I would discourse. [18]
> (I, ll. 663–75)

over what he terms an "eulogium on a self-murderer" (423):

> Oh, ever beauteous, ever friendly! tell
> Is it, in heaven, a crime to love too well?
> To bear too tender or too firm a heart,
> To act a lover's or a Roman's part?
> Is there no bright reversion in the sky,
> For those who greatly think, or bravely die? [19]
> (ll. 5–10)

Samuel Johnson, then, has really no part to play in John Wesley's argument. In fact, had not his *Life of Prior* crossed Wesley's path, or had Wesley not recognized that the essay contained information supplied by Spence and Pope, it is quite likely that *Thoughts on the Character and Writings of Mr. Prior* would not have been written. What *was* written, however, came forth as a reaction (or, perhaps, more of a *reflex* action) to Pope, not to Johnson; for, as indicated earlier, Wesley and Johnson were always on the best of terms. Johnson thought Wesley a good conversationalist, one who could talk well on any subject, and he always respected Methodists for "their expressing themselves in a plain and familiar manner, which is the only way to do good to the common people. . . ."[20] For his part, Wesley held a similar view of Johnson, admiring his *Journey to the Western Islands of Scotland* and his *Taxation No Tyranny*—extracting the latter volume under the title *Calm Address to the American Colonies*. If Johnson knew of Wesley's essay on Matthew Prior, he never mentioned it. In fact, on Thursday, 18 December 1783, almost a year to the day before Johnson's death, Wesley visited him at Bolt Court; they spent two hours together, and Wesley noted that "Dr. Johnson . . . is sinking into the grave by gentle decay."[21] Finally, we will recall that Johnson's closeness with the Wesleys' sister, Mrs. Martha Hall, opened the doors for him at Charles Wesley's home in Chesterfield Street.

In light of literary and personal relationships, it would not be idle diversion to speculate that Wesley intentionally misquoted Johnson to obscure the real identity of both the "ingenious writer" and his essay. He wanted no part of a literary controversy or a personal quarrel with the author of the *Lives of the Poets*; in fact, Wesley owed a debt to Johnson for having turned the other cheek during the storm over the publication of the Methodist leader's *Calm Address*.[22] Although Wesley had really abstracted Johnson's *Taxation No Tyranny*, he never paid rightful tribute to its lawful creator, and an attack by Johnson could have brought about a severe loss of intellectual credibility for Methodism. What Wesley did want, however, was an opportunity to castigate Pope for his "Elegy to the Memory of an Unfortunate Lady," a poem that continued to bother his sense of moral propriety. Wesley's essay, especially at the beginning, is so vague and obscure, and he so manipulates and distorts Johnson's prose throughout, that the careless reader could well have come away with the impression that the "ingenious writer" had merely presented a paraphrase or a re-creation of an earlier discussion of Prior by Pope. Of course, we will never know Wesley's *actual* intentions in this matter. What is obvious, however, is that his *Thoughts upon Prior* represents for him a rare exercise in editorial and critical power.

Chapter Seven

Pedagogical and Linguistic Prose and Poetry

Considering the extent and the depth of the Wesleys' concern for the human condition, it is tempting to construct an image of the two brothers embracing to their bosoms scores of young, cherubic heads or frolicking among the heather and the down, pursued by equal numbers of small but plump figures. However, as we may well imagine, neither had the time for such pleasure; in fact, considering the hardship and the regimen at Epworth rectory, neither had much knowledge of or experience with the sports and diversions of childhood. Nevertheless, both shared a mutual concern for children: their minds, their morals, their Christian attitudes. In the hymns of Charles and the prose of John, there appear repeatedly the notions that Christian training was essential to the development of Christian piety, and Christian discipline, and that young Christian minds were the fields in which to plant the seeds of the Christian life. Indeed, pedagogy became a principal instrument of the eighteenth-century evangelical revival.

As with all other aspects of the Wesleys' evangelical organization, if pedagogy were to have any meaning and thus be effective, it would have to be formalized. For Charles Wesley, the problem *appeared* rather simple: he eventually married and settled in to raise a family; in part, his children's hymns, built somewhat from the foundation established earlier in the century by Isaac Watts, came from a natural inclination toward what he perceived to be the spiritual necessities of children. Had he been left to his own purpose and design, he might have made some contribution to juvenile literature. However, he labored as a complement to the will and the autocracy of his elder brother. John Wesley never really renewed his acquaintance with childhood; his idea of the juvenile world reflected the sharp memories of Epworth and Charterhouse—a world

108

of learning and fairly harsh discipline, of silence and almost blind obedience wherein love and affection rarely displayed themselves in public. Thus John Wesley's pedagogical and linguistic works appear harsh in terms of what we, in the present century, comprehend about education, its purposes and its processes. In addition, his philosophy of education is constructed upon the same religious and moral structure that we find in his literary, theological, and social manifestos. Again, if we can bring ourselves to understand that John Wesley's concern is for a Methodist philosophy of education to educate the children of Methodists, then what he has to say in the following tracts, and what Charles Wesley has to say in his hymns for children, make sense. Finally, we must continue to remember that the prose and poetry discussed below come from two products of the most traditional forms of British education. To the ends of their days, John and Charles Wesley remained students and scholars of the classics; even their fervor for practical Christianity could not erase the imprints of Charterhouse, Westminster School, and Christ Church, Oxford.

On Educating Children

In the *Arminian Magazine* for 1783, John Wesley published an essay of eight paragraphs entitled *A Thought on the Manner of Educating Children*. The piece—a broad statement of the writer's educational philosophy—begins with a veiled reference to a gentleman who objects to the strictness of religious education. Wesley proposes to dwell on the matter, since he "knew it was quite agreeable to the sentiments of Rousseau in his 'Emilius;' the most empty, silly, injudicious thing that ever a self-conceited infidel wrote."[1] Once the rapier has been removed from Rousseau, then Wesley can turn to the issue, a defense of strict religious education according to what he views as the substance of religion, "in holy tempers; in the love of God and our neighbour; in humility, gentleness, patience, long-suffering, contentedness in every condition . . . in the image of God, in the mind that was in Christ . . ." (476). Actually, his definition of education, which grows out of a religious context, is extremely simple; it embodies both meaning and purpose: ". . . to turn the bias from self-will, pride, anger, revenge, and the love of the world, to resignation, lowliness, meekness, and the love of God" (476).

Lessons for Children

In 1746, 1747, and 1748, Wesley published, for the pupils at Kingswood School, near Bristol, an essentially editorial work in three parts entitled *Lessons for Children* (76, 108, and 124 pages, respectively) and extracted almost entirely from the Old Testament. The fifty-four lessons in Part I come from the first five books of Moses; the fifty-four in Part II consist of selections from the time the Hebrews passed over Jordan to the reign of King Hezekiah; the fifty-seven lessons in Part III owe their origin to Ezra, Nehemiah, Job, Psalms, and Proverbs.

Wesley's general preface to the series is an address "To All Parents and Schoolmasters." He declares that the lessons have been made plain and easy, thus requiring little alteration and a minimum of editorial apparatus. The emphasis is to be on comprehension and retention. "Beware," he cautions the masters, "of that common, but accursed, way of making children parrots, instead of Christians. Labour that, as far as it is possible, they may understand every single sentence which they read. Therefore, do not make haste."[2] Thus the children's reading habits must be carefully monitored, and they need to be questioned continually on every point of a given lesson. "If by any means they may not only read, but inwardly digest, the words of eternal life" (217).

The Complete English Dictionary

The attempts of the literati of eighteenth-century Britain to purify and to stabilize the English language can be seen most clearly in the area of lexicography. In one sense, the dictionary was the child of the eighteenth century, an infant that quickly achieved maturity in mid-April 1755 with the publication of Samuel Johnson's *Dictionary of the English Language*. That book made such an impact upon the language—as well as upon its speakers and writers—that it reduced its predecessors and successors to minor accomplishments. That does not mean, however, that those *other* dictionaries lacked effect or influence upon the language. Indeed, Nathan Bailey's *Universal Etymological English Dictionary* (1721) passed through more than twenty-five editions by the century's end, while his *Dictionarium Britannicum* (1730) contained 48,000 entries, provided stress accents and derivations, and included proper names. Benjamin Martin's *Lingua Britannica Reformata* (1749) came forth as the first dictionary in which the meanings of a word were presented in systematic order. Eighteen years after Johnson published his *Dictionary*, William Kenrick gave to the world *A New Dictionary of the English Language, to which is prefixed a Rhetorical Grammar* (1773), a work that generally followed Johnson's etymology, definitions, and illustrations of idiom and phraseology.

Although few people today are aware of the fact, the name of John Wesley belongs to the list of eighteenth-century British lexicographers. In 1753, two years before the publication of Johnson's *Dictionary*, Wesley issued

The Complete English Dictionary, explaining most of those Hard Words which are found in the Best English Writers. By a Lover of Good English, and Common Sense. N.B. The Author assures you, he thinks this is the best English Dictionary in the World. 12vo. 144pp.[3]

The curious title informs us of Wesley's dual purpose for publishing this volume. As we noticed in the preceding chapter, he published, between 1749 and 1755, *The Christian Library: Consisting of Extracts from and Abridgements of, the Choicest Pieces of Practical Divinity;* the *English Dictionary,* then, was intended to explain to humble Methodist readers those words which Wesley had discovered they could not understand. In addition, the Methodist leader wished to provide his followers with an alternative to the errors and the erudition that he believed characterized the efforts of his rivals.

. . . this little Dictionary is not only the shortest and cheapest, but likewise, by many degrees, the most correct, which is extant at this day. Many are the mistakes in all the other English Dictionaries which I have yet seen: Whereas I can truly say, I know of none in this: And I conceive the reader will believe me; for if I had, I should not have left it there. Use, then, this help, till you find a better. (234)

Was Wesley, in company with others interested in language purification and stability, waiting impatiently, in 1753, for the publication of Johnson's volume, the plan of which had appeared in 1749? Or, at age fifty, was he suddenly determined to try his hand at satire, to create a variation of Swift's *Battle of the Books?*

On at least two instances in his preface, at the beginning and at the end (the latter is quoted immediately above), Wesley alludes to the general cheapness of his *Dictionary*—that it will assist the reader "to understand the *best* English authors; and that with as little expense of either time or money as the nature of the thing will allow" (233). To that purpose, he has omitted both highly technical terms and obvious function words *(and, of, but)* that he believes abound in other dictionaries. Then he proceeds to bare his blade:

> I should add no more, but that I have often observed, the only way, according to the modern taste, for any author to procure commendation to his book, is, vehemently to commend it himself. For want of this deference to the public, several excellent tracts, lately printed, but left to commend themselves by their intrinsic worth, are utterly unknown or forgotten: Whereas, if a writer of tolerable sense will but bestow a few violent encomiums on his own work; especially, if they are skillfully ranged in the title page; it will pass through six editions in a trice: The world being too complaisant to give a gentleman the lie; and taking it for granted, he understands his own performance best.   (234)

Strange, that Wesley would have chosen the preface to his *Dictionary* to attack a subject that—although probably worthy of criticism— was only slightly related to lexicography, or at least to helping his Methodist readers to understand the difficult words in works from *The Christian Library*. However, satire or pretension aside, although is volume never passed beyond the first edition, it may be of value if for no other reason than that it contains the first "official" defi- nition of the word *Methodist:* "One that lives according to the method laid down in the Bible."

Grammars

In his *Plain Account of Kingswood School* (1781), John Wesley commented upon what he viewed as a serious gap in the school curricula of the day:

And . . . as to the languages, there are some schools of note wherein no Hebrew at all is taught; and there are exceeding few wherein the scholars are thoroughly instructed even in the Latin and Greek tongues. They are not likely to be; for there is a capital mistake in their very method of teaching. The books which they read are not well chosen, not so much as with regard to language.[4]

Actually, he had taken measures to solve the problem, at least as it concerned his own school at Kingswood. Between 1748 and 1751,

Wesley published his English, Latin, French, Greek, and Hebrew grammars (each of which bore the title *A Short . . . Grammar*) for the use of the young scholars at the institution outside Bristol.

The volumes are really monographs rather than full-length textbooks, for they range in length between eleven and eighty pages. Each follows an obvious pattern, beginning with a section "Of Letters" and moving forward to discussions on the various parts of speech. The sections vary in length, of course, depending upon the complexities—as presented, especially, in Greek and Hebrew. In general, however, the grammars are not exemplars of Wesley's prose style; indeed, they exist as compendiums of linguistic rules and regulations, presented crisply and succinctly. Thus we may note, for examination, an entire "section" from *A Short English Grammar:*

SECTION IV.
Of Verbs.
1. A VERB is a sort of word that expresses either doing, and then it is called an Active; suffering, and then it is called a Passive; or being, and then it is called a Neuter, Verb.
2. Verbs are not only varied by Numbers and Persons, but also by Moods, Tenses, and Conjugations.
3. There are four Moods: (1) The Imperative, which shows that a thing is done: (2) The Indicative, which commands it to be done: (3) The Subjunctive, which generally follows another Verb, and expresses that a thing may, can, or should be done: And, (4) The Infinitive, which has neither Number nor Person.
4. There are five Tenses: (1) The Present Tense, which speaks of the present time: (2) The Preterimperfect, which speaks of the time not perfectly past: (3) The Preterperfect, which speaks of the time perfectly past: (4) The Preterpluperfect, which speaks of the time that is more than perfectly past: And, (5) The Future, which speaks of the time to come.
5. A Conjugation is the manner of varying the beginning or ending of Verbs, in their several Moods.
6. There is but one Conjugation in English.[5]

Hymns for Children

Throughout the eighteenth century, hymns written expressly for or directed to children served, principally, as complements to the pedagogical process, rather than as parts of church liturgy. Until after mid-century, Isaac Watts's *Divine Songs Attempted in Easy Language for the Use of Children* (1715) led the field; basically, the poetry

of the Nonconformist minister of Stoke Newington negated the
solemnities of mature religious thought and emphasized, instead,
the aspects of spiritual delight and moral profit. In other words,
Watts wrote some excellent poetry that accomplished little, theologically, beyond the versification of Puritan moral teaching. Notice, for instance, the second verse from the fourth piece in the 1715
collection, "Whene'er I take my walks abroad":

> Not more than others I deserve,
> Yet God hath giv'n me more;
> For I have food while others starve,
> Or beg from door to door.
> (ll. 5—8)

Almost fifty years after the first edition of Isaac Watts's *Songs for
Children,* Charles Wesley published his *Hymns for Children* (Bristol:
E. Farley, 1763). Of the 105 poetic pieces, five were directed (by
virtue of a section heading) to girls, while an additional twenty-
five appeared under a section entitled "Hymns for the Youngest."
Generally, Wesley intended to continue Watts's design of communicating both the sound and the sense of the verses to the level
of the juvenile mind. He somehow lost sight of that intent, however,
for a large number of his hymns focus upon problems usually reserved
for the mature intellect, as, for example:

> How then ought I on earth to live,
> While God prolongs the kind reprieve,
> And props the house of clay!
> My soul concern, my single care,
> To watch, and tremble, and prepare
> Against the fatal day![6]   (ll. 7—12)

What happened to change the direction of Watts's earlier purpose
for children's hymnody may best be determined by looking at the
preface to John Wesley's revision of his brother's poems, published
in late March 1790:

There are two ways of writing or speaking to children [wrote John
Wesley]: the one is, to let ourselves down to them; the other, to lift them
up to us. Dr. Watts has wrote on the former way, and has succeeded
admirably well, speaking to children as children, and leaving them as he

found them. The following hymns are written[7] on the other plan: they contain strong and manly sense, yet expressed in such plain and easy language as even children may understand. But when they do understand them, they will be children no longer, only in years and in stature.

(*PW*, 6:370)

The final sentence of the above passage clearly indicates, at least as concerned the elder of the two Wesleys, the relationship between hymnody and pedagogy in Methodist thought and practice.

The specifics of that relationship can be viewed, also, in Charles Wesley's dedicatory hymn for the opening of Kingswood School, "Come, Father, Son, and Holy Ghost" (*PW*, 6:407–8, Hymn 40). The poet begins by asking that "The sacred discipline be given, / To train and bring them up for heaven" (ll. 5–6), the training process itself to be governed by the unification of knowledge and piety:

> Learning and holiness combined,
>   And truth and love, let all men see,
> In these, whom up to Thee we give,
> Thine, wholly thine, to die and live.
>
> (ll. 27–30)

In three other hymns (*PW*, 6:421–22, Hymns 52–54)—entitled, simply, "Before School," "In School," and "After School"—Charles Wesley captures the essence of his brother's concerns about the education of youth. His singers ask for "an humble, active mind, / From sloth and folly free," trained to learn "The lessons of Thy love." They search for useful knowledge combined with the ability to "Live to His glory, and declare / Our heavenly Teacher's praise."

What we view in this collection, then, really turns out to be hymns written for students, pupils, scholars or whatever anyone wishes to term them. Unlike Isaac Watts's 1715 *Divine Songs,* in which the singers of all the hymns are clearly identified as *little* boys and *little* girls, Charles Wesley's volume—although not totally unconcerned about youth—does not appear restricted to individuals whose chronological ages identify them as children. Childhood, for Wesley, is undoubtedly that necessary vacuum to be endured by everyone. The real question, simply, is

> When, dear Lord, ah! tell us when
> Shall we be in knowledge men;

> Men in strength and constancy,
> Men of God, confirm'd in Thee?   (*PW*, 6:403)

Thus, when the Methodist poet asks God to "Hear, then, Thy Children's call" (*PW*, 6:416), we cannot always, in confidence, be certain as to exactly whom he has in mind. Little wonder, then, that in terms of pure longevity and overall success in the area of children's hymnody, Watts's *Divine Songs* went through in excess of five hundred imprints in England and America between 1715 and 1915, whereas all that can be said for Charles Wesley's companion volume is that only a small number of the more popular pieces managed to survive, finding places in a variety of British and American hymnals. Nonetheless, during the last three and one-half decades of the eighteenth century, the *Hymns for Children*, as examples of what John Wesley would term *practical poetry*, assisted Methodist youth in formulating their earliest inquiries about *practical* Christianity. For John Wesley, as the Methodist leader most concerned with the education of Methodist children, his brother's poetry could do no more.

Chapter Eight
Political, Historical, and Medical Works

The prose works of John Wesley concerned with politics, history, and medicine demonstrate the influence of the diminutive minister over his Methodist followers. He had such confidence in his ability to direct the minds and the hearts of tens of thousands of Britons that he reacted quickly to the important issues of the moment, trying first to educate his readers and second to form them into a potent social and political force governed by reason and a sense of moral propriety. Such an observation in no way attempts to brand John Wesley a charlatan or a demagogue; he was far too honest to seek anything for his own gain—despite the accusations prevalent in the anti-Methodist broadsides of the day. The greatness of John Wesley results, in part, from his keen sense of responsibility to those whom he served and led. Thus, if the government proved itself incompetent or weak, he owed it to both the governors and the governed to expose the sickness and propose a cure. If those who attacked the government had no right to do so, or if their arguments made no sense, he felt a responsibility to rise in defense of both king and ministry. If the medical profession (or what passed, in the eighteenth century, for the medical profession) failed to serve the needs of the sick, then he owed it to human beings throughout the nation to provide practical and effective means whereby they could learn to care for themselves. He viewed his role neither as a malcontent nor a radical social reformer; instead, Wesley saw himself as a minister of the Gospel who was required, by both Church and Scripture, to refute, when the occasion demanded, what he judged to be unjust.

In the following discussions of selected political, historical, and medical prose tracts, we will often see John Wesley at his rhetorical and stylistic best. He wrestles with problems that are immediately and clearly before him: hunger, poverty, sickness, the past and present states of the kingdom. In so doing he dons a more natural and comfortable habit than when he must appear before the world as a philosopher and a theologian. He may at times inform his readers that he has no bias or favor for one faction or the other, or for one solution over another. Nevertheless, anything that portends harm to people, that appears to threaten the general welfare, causes him to rise in their defense. Thus we can understand the reasons behind the success of eighteenth-century Methodism. For one of the few times in the long history of their nation, certain Britons saw, in John Wesley, not so much a solution to their problems, but a symbol of concern for what they had to endure—a beacon of warmth directed against the cold indifference of the Establishment.

Thoughts on Public Affairs

John Wesley's first political tract, *Free Thoughts on the Present State of Public Affairs. In a Letter to a Friend*, though actually written in December 1768, did not appear in print until 1770. At its most obvious level, the piece represents Wesley's reaction to a personality totally opposite to his own, John Wilkes. After having been expelled from the House of Commons in January 1764 for his attack in the *North Briton* on the government of John Stuart, Lord Bute, he took up residence in Paris; while there, he was tried and found guilty for having published, in 1763, an obscene poem entitled *Essay on Woman*. Returning to England in 1768, Wilkes sought, unsuccessfully, a seat in Parliament for the City of London; he then managed to get himself returned to Commons as M.P. for Middlesex. When the authorities seized him and deposited him in King's Bench Prison, a mob rose in his behalf and rioted for more than a week in May outside the prison and in St. George's Fields. Troops were called to the scene and fired on the crowd, killing six of the rioters and wounding fourteen. After months of courtroom and parliamentary haggling, Wilkes received a prison sentence of twenty-two months and a fine of £1000 for his part in inciting the "Massacre of St. George's Fields." Wilkes built a reputation on what his followers believed to be nothing short of government persecution: neither the ministry nor Commons had the right to determine who should represent Middlesex in Parliament. That obligation belonged to the electorate.

Wilkes proved not to be the only national irritant during 1768. William Pitt the elder, stricken with gout, could not find strength for proper leadership of his two-year ministry. He resigned in October, never more to hold public office. The taxation program for America was causing problems rather than adding gold to the treasury. In May, amidst the Wilkes riots, the French began to negotiate with the Genoese for the purchase of Corsica; the Duke of Grafton complained loudly, but George III wanted no part of hostilities with France. In the autumn, the "Junius" letters appeared in the *Public Advertiser*, inaugurating the inflammatory onslaughts against Grafton and the thirty-year-old king.

Obviously aware of such events and, more important, cognizant of their effect upon the welfare of the nation, John Wesley sought to inject his influence into the sensitive political issues of the moment, to temper the heat of radical rhetoric and to bank the fires of pessimism. He chose the epistolary form, obviously an attempt to follow the pattern and the tone—but certainly not the opinion—of the early Junius. "Only please to remember," he warns his readers, "I do not take upon me to dictate either to you or to any one. I only use the privilege of an Englishman, to speak my naked thoughts; setting down just what appears to me to be the truth, till I have better information."[1] In the style of the political pamphleteer, Wesley feigns neutrality, insisting that his eyes are not blinded by passion; being angry at no one, "I wish the same happiness which I wish to myself, to those on one side and on the other" (15). Thus, for the first nine paragraphs, the Methodist leader plays the kind of rhetorical whist that had been in vogue since the days of Swift's *Modest Proposal*, the only problem being that John Wesley is not Jonathan Swift and the issue, although serious, does not carry the dramatic intensity of an Irish famine.

Nonetheless, once he gets past the introduction, Wesley identifies, in fairly clear terms, the problems and offers equally clear solutions, or at least suggestions for solution. As an individual loyal to the principle of monarchy and to the entire system of parliamentary government, he rushes quickly to defend the traditional institutions of his nation. The natural instinct of the people during periods of public commotion or discontent, maintains Wesley, is to heap blame upon their sovereign. The cry goes up, " 'King George ought to be treated as King Charles was!' Is it the extraordinary bad character of the King? I do not apprehend it is. Certainly, if

he is not, as some think, the best Prince in Europe, he is far from
being the worst" (16). He holds a similar view of the ministers,
who turn out to be "not a jot worse than their opponents, than
those who bawl the loudest against them, either with regard to
intellectual or moral abilities, with regard to sense or honesty" (20).
We recognize easily the chant of mid-century political orthodoxy
sprinkled liberally with doses of Restoration fear. "From plots and
treasons Heav'n preserve my years, / But save me most from my
petitioners!" cries Dryden's David (Charles II) at the end of *Absalom
and Achitophel* (ll. 985–86); Wesley recasts the thought in a less
patient tone: "Let them mind their own work, keep to their pits
and keels, and leave State affairs to me" (19).

The villain of the piece, the cause of all commotion and ferment,
is, of course, John Wilkes. Wesley regards him as a person "en-
numbered with no religion, with no regard to virtue or morality . . ." (26). A politician angry at the world because he has been
denied access to power, Wilkes, in Wesley's view, dons the mask
of the British patriot and thirsts after English as well as French
gold. Thus, ruled by covetousness, ambition, pride, envy, and re-
sentment, Wilkes fans the flames of national unrest. "The madness
becomes epidemic," observes Wesley, "and no medicine hitherto
has availed against it. The whole nation sees the State in danger,
as they did the Church sixty years ago; and the world now wonders
after Mr. Wilkes, as it did then after Dr. Sacheverel" (27).[2]

Wesley moves his *Free Thoughts* toward a conclusion by considering the consequences to the island-kingdom should Wilkes be
permitted to ply his radical trade. As with every staunch Tory, his
thoughts turn back upon the interregnum of more than a century
past. The course of events can easily run from bad to worse; the
nation can become bathed in blood simply because certain individuals would enjoy seeing neighbor pitted against neighbor. "Then,"
declares Wesley, "either a commonwealth will ensue, or else a second
Cromwell. One must be; but it cannot be determined which, King
W——, or King Mob" (28). To restore peace, then, to bring order
back to the land, the king must execute the extant laws against
traitors and incendiaries "to teach them, that there is a difference
between liberty, which is the glory of Englishmen, and licentious-
ness, a wanton abuse of liberty, in contempt of all laws, divine and
human" (33). Had not John Wesley been a Methodist, his words
undoubtedly would have been embraced with utmost warmth by

the Establishment, and he would have been given an equally warm welcome to the highest ranks of Tory conservatism.

Thoughts upon Liberty

The sparks of discontent and general uproar that had so disturbed John Wesley in 1768 showed little signs of diminishing four years later. In 1771, John Wilkes managed to achieve another political triumph, this time as sheriff for London and Middlesex; by 1774, he would become Lord Mayor and reenter Parliament as Member for Middlesex. Further, by the end of 1772, no less than forty-eight different editions of *The Letters of Junius* had already poured from the presses, although only three had been authorized by "Junius" himself.[3] We have already seen, and will see more of, Wesley's reactions to John Wilkes. As far as concerns the author of the Junius letters, Wesley supposedly offered his services to George's ministers for the purpose of authoring the official government responses: "I will show the difference," he reportedly asserted, "between rhetoric and logic."[4] We cannot determine the disposition of the offer; however, Wesley once again shouldered his pen in defense of George III's policies, this time in a tract entitled *Thoughts upon Liberty*, published in 1772 and dated 24 February of that year.

Wesley's purpose is, from the outset, to develop a definition of *liberty*, a concept that he views as "the glory of rational beings."[5] There exist, however, various interpretations both of the context and the meaning of the term. For example, persons in various parts of the world are free to knock others on the head or cut their throats to fulfill their wants; others simply take what they see and what they want; others reach out, at will, for the wives and daughters of their neighbors; still others remove, on a whim, a king whom they believe to be irresponsive to their demands. Wesley then proceeds to consider the divisions of liberty as either *religious* or *civil*. The former he defines as "a liberty to choose our own religion, to worship God according to our own conscience, according to the best light we have" (37). Civil liberty, he maintains, is the opportunity "to enjoy our lives and fortunes in our own way; to use our property, whatever is legally our own, according to our own choice" (41). The necessity for dwelling upon the various contexts and aspects of liberty arose, in part, from Wesley's reaction to a petition, drawn up and presented to Parliament in 1772, signed by 250 clergy and an additional number of lawyers and physicians, requesting relief from having to subscribe to the thirty-nine articles of the Church of England.[6]

Thoughts concerning the Origin of Power

A second political tract published by John Wesley in 1772, *Thoughts concerning the Origin of Power*, exists as a series of circuitous arguments against the idea that the people of a nation constitute the origin of power. If such were the case, according to his reasoning, if the people of every country determined their governors and how they must conduct their affairs, every man, woman, and child would have to be enfranchised, would have to be permitted a part in the constitution of parliaments and the formation of ministries. Wesley argues that those who clamor the loudest for entrusting supreme power in the people are also the ones who rush to restrict the vote to freeholders who have forty shillings per year and who have attained the age of twenty-one years.

The essence of Wesley's own concept of the origin of power lies with his declaration that "I cannot but acknowledge, I believe an old book . . ." (47). Thus he points directly to the opening verse of Paul's epistle to the Romans, Chapter 13: "Let every soul be subject unto the higher powers. For there is no power but of God: the powers that be are ordained of God." Therefore, it is impossible, he contends, to defend the principle that the people are the origin of power, since not *everyone* really has the privilege of selecting those who will govern him. Once more, he returns to the point of origin: the weakness of the democratic scheme is that power belongs only to the few, not to everyone as supposed. "Therefore," he concludes, "this boasted principle falls to the ground, and the whole super-structure with it. So common sense brings us back to the grand truth, 'There is no power but of God'" (53).

Thoughts upon Slavery

Although the name of John Wesley is not to be found among the notables of history who actively opposed slavery and the slave trade in England and America during the eighteenth century, the founder and leader of British Methodism was indeed aware of both of those vile institutions. In fact, as early as April 1737, he viewed firsthand—at Purrysburg, in the South Carolina colony, situated some twenty miles northwest of Savannah—the use of slaves to cultivate the rice crop upon which the economy of the area depended. Even after his return to England, Wesley maintained his contacts with America and was always aware (sometimes more than George III and his ministers) of economic and political developments there. Nonetheless, being far removed from the slavery issue and being deeply involved with social causes of his own, there was little he could do about it, as it pertained either to England or to America. Early in 1772, however, he began to muster his emotions for some form of action against the institution of slavery and its even more inhumane adjunct, the African slave trade. On Wednesday, 12 February 1772, enroute to London from Dorking in Surrey, he read what he termed "a book . . . published by an honest Quaker, on that execrable sum of all villanies, commonly called the Slave-trade. I read of nothing like it in the heathen world, whether ancient or modern; and it infinitely exceeds, in every instance of barbarity, whatever Christian slaves suffer in Mohametan countries."[7]

The book studied by Wesley on the road from Dorking to London came from the pen of Anthony Benezet and bore the title *A Caution to Great Britain and Her Colonies, relative to enslaved Negroes in the British Dominions*. Born in St. Quentin, France, educated in Holland and England, and a resident of Philadelphia from 1731 until his death, this basically gentle Quaker pamphleteer spent the greater part of his life denouncing the iniquity of the slave trade and the cruelty exercised by those in the northern American colonies who purchased and employed Negroes. Five years later he produced another piece, *Some Historical Account of Guinea, with an Enquiry into the rise and progress of the Slave Trade, its nature and lamentable Effects*; together, the tracts ignited the first real flames of the antislavery and anti—slave-trade movements in England and America. In a letter to Lord North, dated 18 February 1772, Granville Sharp, one of the leaders in England in the effort to eradicate the slave trade, indicated that he sent to the prime minister a book "lately printed at Philadelphia, which amongst other things worthy of notice, contains some sensible propositions for *abolishing slavery in the Colonies* . . . that your Lordship may see, the *absolute* necessity of such a measure. . . ."[8] Dr. Benjamin Rush, the Philadelphia chemistry tutor and signer-to-be of the Declaration of Independence, wrote to Sharp on 1 May 1773, noting that "A spirit of humanity and religion begins to awaken, in several of the Colonies, in favour of the poor negroes. The clergy begin to bear a public testimony against this violation of the laws of Nature and Christianity. Great events have been brought about by small beginnings. Anthony Benezet stood alone a few years ago, in opposing negro slavery in Philadelphia; and now three-fourths of the province, as well as of the city, cry out against it. . . ."[9]

After reading Benezet's *Caution to Great Britain* and the *Historical Account of Guinea*, Wesley emerged from his private meditations and published in 1774 what appeared to be his own thoughts on the matter, a tract of twenty-three pages entitled *Thoughts upon Slavery*. However, the small volume actually turned out to be an abridgment of Benezet's *Historical Account of Guinea*, produced in the same manner as *A Calm Address to Our American Colonies* (see next section), a liberal paraphrase of Samuel Johnson's *Taxation No Tyranny*. Lest the Methodist patriarch be branded, too quickly, for plagiarism, we must remember that "abridgments" of others' literary efforts stood as a common practice for him, the simplest and the fastest means by which he could edit for and then disseminate to his followers, especially the less educated and the less enlightened among them, works on the most vital issues of the day. The authors of the originals only rarely became upset over such a practice; Samuel Johnson displayed little concern over the *Calm Address*, while Benezet demonstrated surprising willingness to promote Wesley's production throughout Pennsylvania and New York. Upon receiving a copy of *Thoughts upon Slavery*, the Philadelphia Quaker reprinted the tract at his own expense; that action, if nothing else, demonstrates his devotion to the antislavery movement and his respect for John Wesley's popularity among the American colonists. Benezet communicated his appreciation for Wesley's abridgment through one of his former pupils at Germantown, William Dillwyn, who arrived in England in 1775; twelve years later, Dillwyn joined Granville Sharp and Thomas Clarkson as founders of the London committee for the abolition of the slave trade.

Wesley's chief contribution to Benezet's *Historical Account* was in making the comments and the data of the original meaningful for those Britons unfamiliar with the entire matter of the African slave trade—unfamiliar, some of them, even with the practice of slavery itself. Thus he begins by defining the term: "By slavery, I mean domestic slavery, or that of a servant to a master."[10] However, he quickly differentiates between the condition of enslavement and the supposed "freedoms" enjoyed by domestic servants. The former, according to Wesley, implies an obligation of perpetual bondage, or *service*, over which the slave has no control; everything functions for the benefit of the master, who, in the end, treats all of his holdings alike—both humans and animals. If Wesley's details at the outset of the abridgment appear overly legalistic, it is because he examined first a rather contemporary legal illustration. In 1772, Francis Hargrave, already an eminent lawyer of Lincoln's Inn, distinguished himself by defending, in a habeas corpus case, a Negro slave by the name of James Somerset; both the definition of slavery and the various properties of the term came almost directly from Hargrave's arguments.[11]

In the next section, the *Thoughts* focuses upon the means by which the Negroes were captured, transported, and then treated upon their arrival in America. Wesley dwells upon the methods of kidnapping and the selling, by various chiefs, of their prisoners of war. Again, he relies upon Benezet's own sources—manuscripts of travel narratives—to emphasize the specifics of transactions between tribal chieftains and captains of British slave ships, as well as to communicate the horrors of transporting human cargo across the world: heat, thirst, stench, starvation, exposure, overcrowdedness, all of which reinforce the dehumanization process that places men, women, and children alike on the same level as pack horses and beasts of the field. The conclusion, of course, is that slavery is a violation of natural justice and mercy, a "complicated villany" (70) that cannot be defended, a vile practice brought about by those who seek, at the lowest level of commercial enterprise, nothing but personal wealth under the guise of national benefit. There simply cannot be found on the face of this earth a valid motive for either slavery or the slave trade. "Better no trade," Wesley editorializes, "than trade procured by villany. It is far better to have no wealth, than to gain wealth at the expense of virtue. Better is honest poverty, than all the riches bought by the tears, and sweat, and blood, of our fellow creatures" (74).

A Calm Address to Our American Colonies

Wesley's involvement during the opening months of hostilities in America grew, in part, out of the commitment to advancing the cause of Methodism in that part of the world. The Methodist societies there numbered, by 1774, approximately 2,204 members, ministered to by seven itinerant preachers. Three thousand miles of ocean made control of that body difficult enough; political separation from Great Britain would no doubt carry American Methodists farther away from the influence and direction of their patriarch. However, Wesley's reasons for concern over the situation in America were far from selfish. As late as the middle of June 1775, only forty-eight hours before the battle at Bunker Hill, he attempted to convince the Prime Minster, Lord North, and Lord Dartmouth, Secretary for the Colonies, neither of whom was totally alien to the idea of evangelicalism, that hostilities between Britain and her American colonies would serve no real purpose or solve the difficulties existing between the two parties. In fact, there is evidence that Wesley believed that, in the event of war, the Americans would ultimately gain their independence, depriving Britain of her most valued possessions.[12]

Further, by 1775, Wesley stood at the head of nearly 50,000 British Methodists who, although they had turned away from the religion of their nation, still held firm in their loyalty to the state and to the sovereign. They needed and expected their leader to provide them with the necessary insights into the delicate political situations of the times. Naturally, Wesley believed sincerely in his obligations to his followers, one of which was to understand their sentiments and react accordingly. Thus, when Samuel Johnson set forth his *Taxation No Tyranny; An answer to the Resolutions and Address of the American Congress* in March 1775, Wesley took it upon himself to abridge the tract under the title *A Calm Address to Our American Colonies. By the Rev. Mr. John Wesley, M.A.* The last half of the title proved to be a most unfortunate error in judgment, for it left Wesley open to attacks ranging from plagiarism to senility, weakening what eventually emerged as a basically honest position regarding the American question.

Without dwelling too long upon the substance and method of *Taxation No Tyranny*, it would be fair to state that Johnson, with his usual attention to logic and thoroughness, develops the standard Tory argument as to why the American colonies have no valid right to resist the tax policies of the mother country. All British colonies, maintains Johnson, "however distant, have been, hitherto, treated as constituent parts of the British empire. The inhabitants incorporated by English charters are entitled to all the rights of Englishmen. They are governed by English laws, entitled to English dignities, regulated by English counsels, and protected by English arms; and it seems to follow, by consequence not easily avoided, that they are subject to English government, and chargeable by English taxation."[13] Essentially, Wesley's shorter version paralleled Johnson's thesis of Parliament's right to tax America, contending, as had Johnson, that since large sums of money had been spent in defense of the colonies and of the rights of their inhabitants, it was only reasonable for the Crown to insist that the Americans share the burden. Whether Wesley actually plagiarized Johnson's sentiments is purely academic, since he never intended to write an *original* piece on the subject; the error, of course, involved the placement of his own name on the title-page. At any rate, in terms of the taxation issue itself, both Johnson and Wesley captured the essence of public opinion concerning the matter.

At one point in the abridgment, however, Wesley took his argument half a step beyond that of Johnson. The Methodist leader contended that the militant resistance to British colonial taxation originated not so much with the Americans as it did with "determined enemies to Monarchy" residing in England. In other words, there existed at home a hard core of radicals (obviously Whigs) dedicated to a general undermining of the king and the nation; akin to Milton's Satan, they had managed to steer America to the brink of rebellion, hoping to create an irreparable "breach between England and her colonies." In the end, such madness would bring about the ouster of George and his ministers, to be replaced by "their grand idol, their dear Commonwealth." Wesley bore down upon the idea that the radical Whigs had duped the Americans into playing a key role in the grand scheme of revolution. He pleaded with the colonists to realize where all of the turbulence would lead; the radicals desired only to "play one against the other, in subserviency to their grand design of overturning the English government." In addition, Wesley seemed to recognize that the Americans sought independence from Britain, and thus he argued against the wisdom of that course of action on the grounds that "no subjects are governed in so arbitrary a manner, as those of a Commonwealth."[14]

Finally, Johnson and Wesley differed slightly on the specific measures to be taken by the Crown in preventing both England and America from wallowing in anarchy. Convinced that the colonists had no grounds for rising against the king's taxation policies, Johnson rested his case once more upon the side of reason and order. "Government is necessary to man," he maintained, "and where obedience is not compelled, there is no government. If the subject refuses to obey, it is the duty of authority to use compulsion. Society cannot subsist but by the power, first of making laws, and then of enforcing them."[15] Certainly, Wesley held to the conviction that the Americans had erred by their resistance, but he also continued to believe that, as naive children, they had been led astray by a band of conspirators in England. Thus the leader of the Methodists sought to persuade the colonists that their present course of action would produce one of two obvious results, both of them negative: (1) total subjugation by Britain or (2) independence from the mother nation, which would in turn produce political and economic weakness. Peace and harmony would be restored on both sides of the Atlantic once the colonists reverted to their proper roles as loyal Englishmen and renewed their obligation to fear God and their responsibility to honor their sovereign (87–88).

Some Observations on Liberty

During 1775–1776, public opinion in England concerning the war with the American colonies, although difficult to estimate, appeared fairly well divided. The most outspoken critics of George III's policies were found, according to the historian Lecky, "in the Nonconformist bodies, who were in general earnestly and steadily in favour of the Americans."[16] Thus, in 1776, Richard Price, a Welsh Unitarian residing and preaching at Newington Green, London, published *Observations on the Nature of Civil Liberty, Principles of Government, and the Justice and Policy of the War with America; to which is added an Appendix, containing a State of the National Debt.* Price's tract, a powerful defense of the antiwar forces that related clearly to their cause of constitutional liberty and parliamentary reform, sold 60,000 copies within three months, was almost immediately reprinted in Boston and then, with equal dispatch, translated into Dutch. Finally, it passed through eight editions before America gained its independence. It is a measure of the degree to which the American war had divided the nation that Price, as the result of his *Observations* and two other pamphlets printed in 1777 and 1778,[17] received the appreciation of and a gold snuffbox from the London Corporation, as well as a Doctor of Divinity degree from the University of Glasgow.

Sometime in March 1776, Wesley read Price's *Observations,* and on 4 April he noted that "I began to answer that dangerous tract . . . which, if practised, would overturn all government and bring in universal anarchy."[18] In his thirty-page answer, Wesley takes special care to distinguish between *liberty* and *independence,* stating at the outset that the American colonists had never been denied liberty—physical, moral, religious, or civil. Since, he maintains, there is not a nation on earth whose citizens enjoy *total* liberty, for the supporters of America to declare that the removal of liberty automatically creates slavery appears as mere quibbling over language. For, had not the colonists abused their liberties by not paying the duties established by law, then Parliament would not have removed those liberties. With regard to the persons forced to stand trial for failure to pay the king's duties, Wesley simply inquires into the alternative available. Obviously, in his view, none exists.

> With what justice, then, can this be urged as a violation of their liberty! "O!" cries the man in yon stone doublet, "Bondage! salvery! Help! Englishmen! I am deprived of my liberty!" Certainly you are; but first you deprived the man of his purse.[19]

The remainder of the tract is taken up with issues already familiar to readers of *Thoughts concerning the Origin of Power, Thoughts on Liberty,* and *A Calm Address.* Individuals lawfully born under the government of a nation, even though they may reside elsewhere, remain subjects of that nation; liberty is an empty term for those who cry the loudest, yet who also deny it to others (women, children, and men without property or sufficient income). "You affirm," Wesley tells both Price and his American friends, "all power is derived from the people; and presently exclude one half of the people from having any part or lot in the matter" (102). What really bothers Wesley, however, is what he terms the incendiary nature of Price's arguments, flames of revolution intended to cause harm both to America and to England. He concludes, then, by calling upon all Britons, those who are "real lovers of their country," to douse the fires of anarchy lapping around the feet of king and government.

A Calm Address to the Inhabitants of England

John Wesley continued his rhetorical involvement with the American war in 1777 by publishing *A Calm Address to the Inhabitants of*

England. In that twenty-five-page tract, he begins by dwelling upon the success of his earlier piece, the *Calm Address to the American Colonies:* " . . . within a few months, fifty, or perhaps an hundred thousand copies, in newspapers and otherwise, were dispersed throughout *Great-Britain* and *Ireland.* The effect exceeded my most sanguine hopes."[20] Such acceptance has encouraged Wesley to "address myself once more, not indeed to my Countrymen afar off, but to you who remain in your native land, who are inhabitants of *Old England"* (4).

Wesley then turns his attention to the origin and development of the American revolution, beginning with the year 1737. Charles Wesley, then on his return from Savannah to England, was detained at Boston, where he overheard talk of independence and revolution. However, any loss of liberty that followed—press, religion, or civil rights—came not from a British Parliament, but as the result of "A new Supreme Power called a *Congress.* . . . It openly assumed the reins of Government; exercised all the rights of Sovereignty, burst all the bands, and totally disclaimed all the authority both of King and Parliament" (11). This Congress, he maintains, wields absolute power over those whom it governs, and thus independence has given the colonists not liberty, but autocracy. In England, to the contrary, "it is impossible to conceive a fuller Liberty than we enjoy, both as to Religion, Life, Body, and Goods" (18). Wesley concludes by pointing a stern finger in the direction of "you who are vulgarly called *Methodists"* (21). In short, he warns that if any among them blaspheme God or the king, or even associate with those who do, he will cast them out: "I would no more continue in fellowship with those, who continued in such a practice, than with whoremongers, or sabbath-breakers, or thieves, or drunkards, or common-swearers" (21). After reading both this "calm" address and the 1776 *Reasonable Address,* one might conclude that if John Wesley is deserving of the name *enthusiast,* the award must be presented for his political enthusiasm, not necessarily his religious zeal.

Concise History of England

Toward the end of January 1776, John Wesley had finished his four-volume *A Concise History of England, from the Earliest Times, to the Death of George II,* the preface of which is dated 10 August 1775.

By his own admission, the project was hardly an original work, but contains, instead, "the substance of the English History, extracted chiefly from Dr. Goldsmith, Rapin, and Smollett, only with various corrections and additions."[21] Wesley's purpose in abridging the historical works of others is not necessarily to provide new information, but to present a different set of historical priorities. The extant histories of England, he complains, contain an abundance of unnecessary information; they fail to place the proper emphasis on the material and to inform the reader what is and what is not important; generally, they reflect their authors' lack of judgment, sense, and impartiality. Above all else, however, hovers Wesley's own grand design for English historical prose: "Let there be at least one History of England which uniformly acknowledges this ["that the Lord is King"]; let there be one Christian History of what is still called (though by a strong figure) a Christian country" (275).

From the outset, at least, there seemed to have been a number of people in England who agreed with Wesley's criticisms of British historical writing. The earliest printing of the *Concise History* yielded a profit of £200 for its author/compiler. According to Thomas Olivers, one of Wesley's early preachers who later succeeded to the managership of the profitable Methodist book concern, John Wesley gave away the entire sum within a week's time.[22] In any event, after the apparent novelty had worn away, Wesley's attempts to "Christianize" British history gave way to the more conventional approaches to historiography, and his *Concise History* drifted off upon the large ocean of literary obscurity. However, we need to be reminded of the existence of such a work, since it serves as one more example of the extent to which John Wesley labored to open the sluices of knowledge for the benefit of the unenlightened members of his evangelical organization.

Primitive Physick

John Wesley's campaign to relieve the physical suffering of the poor began in 1746, the same year in which he instituted the lending-stock at the Foundery, Upper Moorfields, to ease the financial burdens of his London converts. Armed with a generous supply of pills, nostrums, and elixirs—in addition to £30 with which to replenish his inventory—Wesley proceeded to dispense, free of charge to those who came to the Foundery, both remedies and medical advice. "I found," he noted in his journal for 6 June 1747, "there had been about six hundred in about six months. More than three hundred of these came twice or thrice, and we saw no more of them. About twenty of those who had constantly attended did not seem to be either better or worse. Above two hundred were sensibly better, and fifty-one thoroughly cured."[23] The success of the scheme—successful in terms of the sheer numbers who came to Upper Moorfields for aid—led Wesley to establish at Bristol, late in 1746, a dispensary for two hundred patients. As a result of the two projects, or, perhaps, because of them, the leader of British Methodism determined to disseminate his medical empirics throughout the kingdom; in fact, in the year previous, he had already published a seventeen-page, two-penny tract entitled *A Collection of Receits for the Use of the Poor*. On 11 June 1747, he issued the first edition of an expanded version of that work, the 119-page *Primitive Physick; or, an easy and natural Method of Curing Most Diseases*.

While *Primitive Physick* cannot be catalogued as a classic of British medical literature, it must certainly be identified as one of the most popular volumes published in England during the eighteenth century. At the time of its author's death on 2 March 1791, the work had reached its twenty-third London edition; a so-called "new edition" appeared in 1828, and a "revised" version—the thirty-sixth edition—came forth in 1840. In America, principally because of Wesley's popularity in that part of the world, the twelfth, thirteenth, fourteenth, sixteenth, and twenty-second editions were reprinted at Philadelphia between 1764 and 1791. And, as late as 1858, the Rev. William Mason Cornell, M.D.—himself author of several tracts on consumption and epilepsy—published, at Boston, a "revised and enlarged" edition of *Primitive Physick*. Wesley's own journals and letters reveal that he updated the remedies and rewrote the prefaces in October 1755, November 1760, April 1780, and May 1781. An interesting footnote on the popularity of the work comes forth in a letter from Wesley to the *London Gazetteer,* dated 28 December 1775, in which he attempts to impress upon the printer that "Between twenty and thirty editions of the *Primitive Physick* . . . have been published either in England or Ireland."[24] Obviously, the Methodist patriarch may have been guilty of wishful thinking, since the *seventeenth* London edition is dated 1776; the Irish "editions" were nothing more than reprints of previous issues.

In his preface to the first edition, Wesley carefully outlines the major reasons for the existence of his *Primitive Physick*. At the most fundamental level—for in almost everything, as we have seen, John Wesley aims for the fundamental—the seeds of wickedness, pain, sickness, and death reside permanently within the frame of mortal man, the price he must pay for having rebelled against his Creator. "The sun and moon shed unwholesome influences from above; the earth exhales poisonous damps from beneath; the beasts of the field, the birds of the air, the fishes of the sea, are in a state of hostility; the air itself that surrounds us on every side, is replete with shafts of death; yea, the food we eat daily saps the foundation of that life which cannot be sustained without it."[25] Historically, maintains the author, man has sought the means to relieve or to lessen the pain and the sickness to which he is naturally and continually exposed; the ancients practiced a simple but effective method of physic, whereby fathers handed down remedies to their sons, who turned them over to their sons, while, at the same time, neighbors shared treatments with one another. Unfortunately, in Wesley's view, the philosophers then entered upon the scene, complicating the issue with inquiries, theories, and a plethora of complex and speculative remedies stuffed into a more than adequate supply of medical books; "at length, physick became an abtruse science, quite out of the reach of ordinary men" (13), while physicians elevated themselves to positions of esteem and removed themselves from those who needed them the most. Thus, styling himself a lover of mankind, which indeed he was, the Methodist leader proposes to reduce physic to its ancient standard, to remove it from the realm of mystery and return it to the most basic level of human understanding so that "every man of common sense, unless in some rare case, may prescribe either to himself or neighbour; and may be very secure from doing harm, even when he can do no good" (14).

On the surface, the more than eight hundred suggestions for 288 "diseases" (beginning with *abortion* and ending with *a wound that is closed too soon*) set forth in the major section of this volume appear, to the twentieth-century readers, nothing more than a collection of old wives' tales blended with a generous dosage of anecdotes that Wesley may well have gathered while among the Indians of Georgia. Nonetheless, if we acclimate ourselves to the language of medicine as practiced in eighteenth-century Britain, certain of the concoctions prove to be valid. For instance, Wesley suggests a diet of milk,

water, turnips, carrots, and bread for preventing "extreme fat";
syringing the ear with warm water to remove excessive wax; keeping
a piece of barley sugar or sugar candy constantly in the mouth to
eliminate "a tickling cough"; milk, milk porridge, and water gruel
as a proper breakfast for children; stewed prunes, water gruel with
currants, or bran as means of relieving "costiveness"; preventing
piles by "washing the parts daily with cold water."[26] Other suggestions loom large from those pages as total absurdities—for example, the remedies for lunacy:

> Give decoction of agrimony four times a day.
> Or, rub the head several times a day with vinegar in which ground-ivy
> leaves have been infused.
> Or, take daily an ounce of distilled vinegar.
> Or, boil the juice of ground-ivy with sweet oil and white wine into
> ointment. Shave the head, anoint it therewith, and chafe it every other
> day for three weeks. Bruise also the leaves and bind them on the head,
> and give three spoonsful of the juice, warm, every morning.
> This generally cures melancholy.
> The juice alone taken twice a day will cure.
> Or, be electrified. (Tried.)   (87)

Yet, given the eighteenth-century's ignorance of and attitude toward
melancholia, or of mental illness in general, Wesley's offerings proved
not substantially different from the opinions of contemporary physicians and theorists. Dr. George Cheyne, writing to the novelist
Samuel Richardson in May 1739 relative to Richardson's lowness
of spirits and bad appetite, advises him that "All Chronical Cases
require Time, Patience, and Perseverance in a proper Method. When
you have read and considered my Essay about a Regimen I believe
you will be directed in the most proper Method to lengthen your
useful Life and to preserve cheerful Spirits, at least I think it the
best known to me or discoverable by Art: the rest we must submit
to Heaven."[27]

Wesley brings his handbook of practical medicine to a close with
a short appendix headed, simply, "Medicines." Here, of course, he
attempts to provide the recipes for those compounds cited most
often throughout the main body of his text: Daffy's elixir, Tur-
lington's balsam, emetic tartar vomit, eye-water, Scotch pills. In
addition, he lists several of the more popular terms—cold-bathing,
water-drinking, electrifying, fasting spittle—and then, for each,

provides an alphabetical roster of disorders that can be remedied by that particular compound. Thus, cold bathing runs the course from apoplexy to want of sleep, water-drinking from apoplexy to trembling, electrifying from St. Anthony's Fire to weakness of the legs, fasting spittle from asthma to warts. Of all those cures, electrifying immediately engages our attention, for its various possibilities never ceased to fascinate the ever-curious Wesley. His interest in its potential began in October 1747, when he first viewed some electrical experiments in London; in February 1753, he read Benjamin Franklin's *Experiments and Observations on Electricity,* remarking, "What an amazing scene is here opened for after-ages to improve upon!"[28] By November 1756, he had procured an electrical machine and proceeded (at Southwark, the Foundery in Upper Moorfields, and Seven Dials) to electrify those suffering from a variety of illnesses. Then, in 1760, seven years before his rival Priestley was to issue the *History and Present State of Electricity* (1767), he published his *Desideratum; or, Electricity made Plain and Useful. By a Lover of Mankind and Common Sense.* Little wonder, then, that he prescribes the treatment on forty-nine different occasions in *Primitive Physick,* concluding that he has never "known one single instance wherein it has done harm; so that I cannot doubt the veracity of those who have affirmed the contrary" (140).

As with his diaries, journals, and sermons—as well as literally hundreds of theological, pedagogical, and historical tracts—John Wesley directed his handbook on the practice of medicine to a wide audience; in so doing, he chose the vehicles of directness, simplicity, and pure practicality. Nevertheless, despite its obvious emphasis upon matters of the body—matters pertaining to preserving the *lives* of his fellow men—Wesley could not keep his *Primitive Physick* entirely free from what was, for him, the most important area of concern: the *soul* of man. Therefore, the only single remedy in which he could place his absolute faith becomes, really, the essence of the piece. "Above all," he asserts, "add to the rest, for it is not labour lost, that old-fashioned medicine—*prayer;* and have faith in God, who 'Killeth and maketh alive, who bringeth down to the grave and bringeth up (18).' " Essentially, that "old-fashioned medicine" became the key to the popularity of the small book, for throughout the volume, its author conveyed the idea that he knew nothing more than that certain maladies *might* be cured by certain reasonable suggestions. He had consulted a number of sources, common sense, and his own experience, tempering those with the general principle of "doing good to all men," particularly "those who desire to live according to the gospel. . . ."[29] One prominent historian of eighteenth-century England refers to Wesley's book as "an absurd, fantastic compilation of uncritical folk-lore."[30] From a purely medical standpoint, especially from the perspective of the twentieth century, such a statement may well be accurate. However, John Wesley's own prescription for life—his complete faith in the gospel—had at least as much to do with the spread of *Primitive Physick* throughout eighteenth-century Britain and America as did all of the remedies and suggestions imprinted upon its pages.

Chapter Nine

Some Literary Reactions to Methodism

The extent to which the Methodist movement directed itself to improving social as well as spiritual conditions in eighteenth-century Britain has not always, if indeed ever, been fully appreciated by or communicated effectively to a broadly based intellectual audience. When John and Charles Wesley established the first truly Methodist society in Bristol early in 1739, both the Anglican Church and the congregations of Protestant Dissent were mired deeply in spiritual lethargy and social apathy. The heralds of rationalism, led by such churchmen as Joseph Butler, Bishop of Bristol, loudly proclaimed the predominance of conscience over human action; their orthodoxy transformed Christianity into a sterile system of morality, supported by divine sanctions. Anglican clerics lulled their parishioners to sleep with sermons on moral virtues and heavenly rewards, seemingly unaware of and unconcerned for those who never heard or never cared to hear them. The entire nation appeared shocked by the vulgar habits and amusements of the poor, the widespread illiteracy among them, the high rates of disease and mortality, the stinking and savage states of existence within the numerous poverty pockets of the larger cities. Yet few put forth any legitimate efforts to alleviate such conditions. To make matters worse, England stood poised to enter upon the industrial revolution, armed with the latest weapons of modernity: steam engine, spinning jenny, power loom. And, as usual, progress was to leave its scars upon those who already had sunk to the lowest depths of spiritual, social, and economic despair.

Certainly, the Wesleys and their Methodist followers were neither saints nor saviors, but at least they stretched forth their hands into corners of British society where none seriously had ventured before them. More than sixty years ago, S. Parkes Cadman, a respected commentator on ecclesiastical history, summarized, somewhat poetically, John Wesley's purpose (although he could just as easily have included Charles): "Undeterred by the appalling contrasts between his tastes and habits and those of the degraded masses . . . [Wesley] entered the dreary haunts of physical and moral destitution, a spiritual Archimedes, who had found his leverage and proposed to upraise the lost and abandoned, not only to decency, but to holiness. He foresaw, gathered from those waste places, an ideal Church of regenerated souls, broadly and securely based on love and social duty."[1] That sense of mission, in addition to the barriers placed before it, may well identify the Methodist movement as one of the most dramatic of the social changes occurring in England between 1739 and 1790. Denied access to Anglican churches, the Wesleyan and Whitefield Methodists took to the open fields, and there reached the hearts and minds of tens of thousands more than would have been possible under more conventional circumstances. Unable to draw freely from the ranks of Anglican clerics sympathetic toward evangelical reform, or even to ordain those within his own ranks, John Wesley developed a corps of lay preachers (both male and female); those he recruited from various social classes, from among the learned and the undereducated. The overall emotionalism generated by the movement outraged men of reason, forced them into the consideration that eighteenth-century man might not be so rational as generalized and popular ideas tried to make him. Through the early development and eventual establishment of Methodism, the Wesleys posed a key question before their contemporaries: Was the Church of England, in its traditional form, capable of coming to grips with the problems created by social and economic change?

Naturally, those among the enlightened establishment who refused to confront the implications of such a question, who cared only to maintain the current level of spiritual and social conservatism, expended considerable labor in their attempts to beat back the challenge. Thus, opposition to Methodism in eighteenth-century Britain assumed three distinct forms: as mentioned, Anglican bishops prohibited Methodist preachers from conducting services in Anglican churches; mobs, instigated by local vicars, rioted at society meetings, while the magistrates issued warrants for the impressment of Methodist preachers; and, beginning about 1739 and continuing even into the nineteenth century, a steady stream of anti-Methodist pamphleteers poured forth invective and twisted biblical evidence in an effort to expose what they generally concluded to be political traitors, religious heretics, and empty-headed enthusiasts. Such opposition, though achieving temporary success through various sanctions, never really achieved its desired end: to slow the advance of and then terminate the movement. When the rains and snow of late fall and winter curtailed field-preaching, the Wesleys retreated to their own chapels and meeting houses throughout the kingdom. And, at the risk of oversimplification, the scurrilous anti-Methodist broadsides amounted to little more than puddles of sour prose and second-rate rhyme from the pens of Establishment loyalists: Thomas Whiston, Zachary Grey, Aquila Smith, William Bowman, Joseph Trapp, Daniel Waterland, William Fleetwood, Evan Lloyd, Joseph Hart, Arthur Bedford, John Parkhurst, Thomas Green, Thomas Griffith, Alexander Jephson, John Langhorne.

As one illustration of anti-Methodist attack on that level, we may consider Evan Lloyd's satire of over one thousand lines entitled *The Methodist. A Poem* (London: Printed for the Author, 1766). Rather than wildly sustaining cannonades of invective upon the backsides of his antagonists, the satirist begins with the broader view; for a moment, at least, his method appears to differ sharply from the general plans employed by his colleagues. For Lloyd, at the outset of his poem, Methodism exists simply as a part of a larger and more serious danger: the decline of reason leads to the overall corruption of the nation. He mourns early the loss of respect for tradition and for the establishment; in a word; "Sense grows diseas'd, and Reason mad."[2] This, naturally, leads to general chaos, a state of corruption wherein

> Tories to Whigs convert, and Whigs,
> Mere Ministerial Whirligigs,
> Turn'd by the hand of Int'rest take
> The Tory-part, for Lucre's sake.
> Patriots turn Placemen, and support
> Against their Country's good the Court;
> Are brought with Pensions to retire,
> When drooping Kingdoms most require
> Their aid— (13–14)

From the chaos at that level, the poet turns his attention to an assault on religion by no less an arch-foe than Satan, who ascends to earth in search of an "Agent suited to his Mind, / Who cou'd transact his Business Well, / And do on Earth the work of Hell" (23). At that point, the attack upon Methodism and on the corruption it supposedly causes increases in intensity; Lloyd essentially falls back upon the hackneyed arguments that generally characterized the efforts of so many of the anti-Methodist diatribes. Satan's agent, a Methodist of "A thousand scorching Words" (27), is guilty of the vilest acts in the name of religion:

> Virgins he will seduce astray,
> Only to shew the shortest Way
> To Heaven, and because it lies
> Above the Zodiac in the Skies,
> That they may better see the Track,
> He lays them down upon their Back. (27)

There follow bombasts, equally as harsh, against John Wesley's program of lay preachers, his publications on science and medicine, Martin Madan's sermons to the patients of the Lock Hospital (whom he served as chaplain), William Romaine's treatises on faith, and the money donated to and the chapels built for the cause by the Countess of Huntingdon. In essence, all Methodists are "Knaves / That crawl on Earth," "Prudes that crowd to Pews, / While their Thoughts ramble to the Stews"; the group boasts "The Names of all the Fools in Town" (48).

Perhaps the single original quality in Lloyd's *The Methodist* can be found in the conclusion to the satire. The poet abruptly breaks off his invective and seemingly apologizes for what he has written:

> Thou God of Truth and Love! excuse
> The honest Anger of the Muse,
> Warm in thy Cause, while She wou'd pray
> That Thou from Earth wou'd'st sweep away
> Such rotten saints, who wou'd conceal
> Their Fraud beneath the name of Zeal!
>   (50)

His technique here is obvious. Through his harsh language and inconsistent couplets, Lloyd has sought to convince his readers that he has become as disorderly, as corrupted, as that which he has criticized for its chaotic and corruptive influences. Here we may observe the role of the persona, as employed so well by Swift in *A Modest Proposal*, although Lloyd does not want to be as subtle as the Irish Dean. Nonetheless, the anti-Methodist poet doggedly pursues his purpose, begging his muse to "Turn not Religion's Milk to Gall! / Let not thy Zeal within thee nurse / A holy Rage, or pious Curse!" (53). The world of order, the established and the rational world, has been taught by God to live in peace with its enemies, to forgive that which seeks to destroy it:

> Live then ye Wretches! to declare,
> How long our God with Men can bear!
> A living Monument to be
> Of the Almighty's Clemency!
> Who still is good, altho' You preach
> Yourselves almost 'bove Mercy's reach;
> And, tho' his goodness You resist,
> Can even spare a Methodist. (54)

And so the poem terminates not with the tears of despair—which would serve only to carry the day for spiritual enthusiasm and social corruption—but upon the vibrant note of harmony. God's well-ordered frame remains whole.

We need clearly to understand, however, that reaction to Methodism and to its leaders was not, during the mid and late-eighteenth century, the exclusive property of pamphleteers or Anglican clergymen; nor, for various reasons, was the reaction always *totally* negative. The *literati* and persons possessed of considerable wit contributed thought-provoking and varied points of view to the discussion. For example, Samuel Johnson had serious doubts concerning both the objectives and propriety of Methodism, primarily because of its political disagreements with the Church of England and its questioning of traditional values. According to James Boswell, "He owned that the Methodists had done good, had spread religious impressions among the vulgar part of mankind, but he said they had great bitterness against other Christians, and that he never could get a Methodist to explain in what he excelled others; that it ended in the indispensable necessity of hearing one of their preachers; that although the same prayers were admitted by the Methodist to be read at church, and the same doctrines to be preached, as in his meeting, still a man could not be right unless he heard a Methodist clergyman."[3] Outright ridicule is absent from Johnson's reaction to

Methodism; he admittedly made no attempt to understand its principles or its social mission. He did believe that the movement
directed itself to negating the earthly productivity of human beings,
thus defying reason and good sense, while debasing human nature.
However, Johnson never doubted the genuineness of Methodism's
leaders; in fact, he rather admired the success of its preachers,
concluding upon one occasion that George Whitefield's popularity
"is chiefly owing to the popularity of his manner. He would be
followed by crowds were he to wear a night-cap in the pulpit, or
were he to preach from a tree."[4] And, as a man of sound judgment,
Johnson could readily perceive the reasons for the apparent success
of Methodism. Again, its preachers and principal advocates could
express themselves "in a plain and familiar manner, which is the
only way to do good to the common people, and which clergymen
of genius ought to do from a principle of duty, when it is suited
to their congregations; a practice, for which they will be praised by
men of sense."[5] We may not be too far from the mark in observing
that beneath Johnson's rather positive reaction to the Methodists'
treatment of the lower classes lies the wish that the Anglican churchmen might incline themselves toward a similar direction.

A decidedly different attitude exists in the efforts of Laurence
Sterne, the Yorkshire cleric turned writer, who represents accurately
the extremes in techniques employed to assault, rhetorically, the
threats to an enlightened England posed by Methodism. In *The
Sermons of Mr. Yorick*, 1760, he simply and directly likens Methodist
preachers to illiterate mechanics who appear more capable of *making*
pulpits than occupying them. His metaphor may well constitute an
example of high wit, yet it is certainly no more or less stinging
than the thousands of other abusive epithets hurled at Methodist
lay preachers of the period. If anything, Sterne demonstrates a sense
of restraint in contrast to Evan Lloyd, who is beside himself at the
prospect of John Wesley's innovation:

> Hence ev'ry Blockhead, Knave, and Dunce,
> Start into Preachers all at once.
> Hence Ignorance of ev'ry size,
> Of ev'ry shape Wit can devise,
> Altho' so dull it hardly knows,
> Which are its Fingers, which its Toes.
> *(The Methodist*, 29)

At the other extreme, Sterne literally challenges the reader's knowledge to discover the true meaning behind this statement in *Tristram
Shandy* (1762): "*Slawkenbergius* was play'd upon, for aught I know,
like one of *Whitefield's* disciples,—that is, with such a distinct
intelligence . . . of which the two masters it was, that had been
practicing upon his *instrument*,—as to make all reasoning upon it
needless."[6] To appreciate fully the abstract but terribly obscene
analogy of George Whitefield and the Methodist preachers to Sterne's
mythical author of a treatise upon noses is to understand the care
with which the novelist coined a label for his fictional essayist, *Hafen
Slawkenbergius*. The Christian name *Hafen* is of course German for
"haven" or "receptacle"—or, in the colloquial, *chamberpot*; for the
surname, Sterne Latinized the German *Schackenberg*: a mountain of
slag, offal, or (again, in the colloquial) *excrement*. Turning from the
essayist to the subject of his tract, the *nose*, we need to be aware of
the traditional belief, widespread during the eighteenth century, in
the size of the penis being proportional with the size of the nose.
The vulgar parallel is maintained not only throughout the Slawkenbergius tale (Volume VI), but in various references to him and
to his treatise prior to the actual relating of the "Slawkenbergii
Fabella." Thus, although the allusion serves to heighten Sterne's
blatant disgust with Methodist principles and practices, the novelist
goes out of his way to obscure his prejudice behind a thick screen
of wit and burlesque. However, once the reader, especially one
strongly supportive of the Establishment, recognizes the object of
this intellectual game, he is, hopefully, shocked into sharing Sterne's
point of view.

Perhaps the most interesting attitude toward Methodism by a
cultivated writer appears in Tobias George Smollett's *Humphry
Clinker*, published in 1771, some three months before the novelist's
death. Plainly, the novel is a humorous piece of fiction; caught up
in spasms of laughter, the audience may have some difficulty de-
termining when Smollett wishes to be serious or when he desires
merely to enjoy an extremely good time at the expense of his characters. Undoubtedly, all is not fun and games for the creator of
these sparkling epistles; rather, he reflects generally the late-eighteenth-century position of reconciliation with and guarded tolerance
of those concepts that had been, for the past several decades, shaking
traditional institutions. For does not his hero, a Methodist, turn
out, in the end, to be the illegitimate son of a gentleman? Is not

Matthew Lloyd, *né* Humphry Clinker, welcomed by his new relatives (his former masters) with open arms, warm hearts, and a new suit of clothes? Yet this is not entirely surprising in view of Matthew Bramble's earlier benevolence upon discovering his lackey, Clinker, preaching at a Methodist meeting. "—What right has such a fellow as you to set up for a reformer? [asks Bramble.]" "Begging your honour's pardon, (replied Clinker) may not the new light of God's grace shine upon the poor and ignorant in their humility, as well as upon the wealthy, and the philosopher in all his pride of human learning?" "What you imagine to be the new light of grace, (said his master) I take to be a deceitful vapour, glimmering through a crack in your upper story—In a word, Mr. Clinker, I will have no light in my family but what pays the king's taxes, unless it be the light of reason, which you don't pretend to follow."[7]

Bramble then proclaims Humphry unfit for his service, informing him that he will eventually end "with a dark room and clean straw in Bedlam," or, perhaps, "hang yourself in despair" (127). At that point, the servant undergoes immediate repentance and begs his master to reconsider. "The squire could not help smiling at the poor fellow's simplicity, and promised to take care of him, provided he would mind the business of his place, without running after the new-light of methodism. . ." (127). But the issue does not end there. Bramble's sister, Tabitha, herself a member of Clinker's short-lived Methodist society, upbraids the young man for want of courage and conscience; whereupon, Bramble proposes that if Humphry cannot "live with me upon such terms as I have prescribed, the vineyard of methodism lies before you, and she [Tabitha] seems very well disposed to regard your labour—" (128). Once more Clinker affirms his dedication to his master, who promises to retain him, at least for a probationary period. Finally, Bramble asks his youthful and misguided servant how he came to discover Methodism. Clinker replies that he "had his devotion kindled by Mr. W—'s preaching: that he was confirmed in this new way, by the preacher's sermons, which he bought and studied with great attention. . ." (128).

In true Smollett fashion, the incident concludes not with the simple resolution of Clinker's conversion through reading sermon literature; it evolves into a large matter. The lackey is not really the prime convert to Methodism. Tabitha Bramble and her niece, Liddy Melford, had taken Lady Griskin and Ralph Barton to hear

Whitefield (or Wesley?) preach on the occasion of Clinker's conversion. Barton had his eyes upon Liddy; Tabitha, with help from Lady Griskin, cast designs upon Barton; Bramble would like nothing better than to see his sister married. The key convert to Methodism, then, is not Clinker, but Barton; Methodism becomes the means "which would occasion a connexion of souls that might be easily improved into a matrimonial union" (129). Thus, upon two occasions in the novel, certain of Smollett's characters openly embrace, accept as a fact of life, a movement to which their creator was obviously hostile. Approximately ten years earlier, in his *Complete History of England* (1757–1758, 1760–1765), he had penned a spirited attack against the Methodist leadership, an opinion noted by John Wesley on Thursday, 22 April 1779, and entered into his journal while he was at Otley: "I was a little surprised at a passage in Dr. Smollett's *History of England*, vol. xv, pp. 121, 122:

Imposture and fanaticism still hang upon the skirts of religion. Weak minds were seduced by the delusions of a superstition, styled Methodism, raised upon the affectation of superior sanctity, and pretensions to divine illumination. Many thousands were infected with this enthusiasm by the endeavours of a few obscure preachers, such as Whitefield, and the two Wesleys, who found means to lay the whole kingdom under contribution.

Poor Dr. Smollett! Thus to transmit to all succeeding generations a whole heap of notorious falsehoods!"[8]

Yet the novelist had at least two reasonable motives for this seeming shift from the harsh opinions expressed in the *History of England* to the off-handed tolerance which he humorously illustrated in *Humphry Clinker*. First, Smollett's primary concern in the latter effort was for the development of his fiction: the epistolary form required careful attention to transition and delineation, as his readers were directed from one letter to the next, from one point of view to another. The institutions of society may have been scoffed at, but for the sake of unity, the novelist attempted to blend the current "-isms" into a larger problem—in this particular instance, Smollett's humor, his characters, and the vision of his native Scotland. And, as the concern for Scotland became more intense, it gave rise to the second reason for Smollett's apparent toleration of Methodism. Unlike the *English* Establishment, Scotland had nothing to fear from Methodism. Although *technically* not Dissenters, English Methodists stood perilously close to separation from the Anglican Church; only John Wesley kept the scattered societies within the Establishment. But in Scotland, *Anglicans* were the dissenters and the disenfranchised; *Anglicans* found themselves subordinate to the Established Church of Scotland, Presbyterian. Simply, Smollett and his fellows north of the River Tweed possessed none of the fears and evidenced none of the violent reactions of the English; the Kirk looked upon Anglicans and Methodists with equal contempt. Certainly, in *Humphry Clinker*, Smollett was not prepared to acknowledge the labors of Whitefield or the Wesleys, nor was he ready to admit to their legitimacy. However, there remains little doubt that between 1765 and 1771, the Scottish novelist had come—in the guise of his character, Matthew Bramble—to recognize Methodism and its preachers as irritating facts of life.

Two successful wits of the period, the novelist Henry Fielding and the actor-dramatist Samuel Foote, prefer to do away with the subtle insinuations or even highly farcical situations when criticizing Methodism. The former, in *Joseph Andrews* (1742), set forth the usual arguments against the enthusiasm of George Whitefield and his converts. Parson Abraham Adams, who pronounces himself a "great . . . enemy of the luxury and splendour of the clergy," was, at one time, an admirer of Whitefield. However, when the popular field-preacher "began to call nonsense and enthusiasm to his aid, and set up the detestable doctrine of faith against good works, I was his friend no longer; for surely that doctrine was coined in hell; and one would think none but the devil himself could have the confidence to preach it."[9] Such an attitude requires no explication; in fact, at this point in the discussion of anti-Methodism in certain literary works, it is almost redundant. Yet, what is actually said is not as important as who has said it.

Fielding depicts Abraham Adams as the naive and quixotic agent of the provincial wing of the Church of England. This essentially honest but terribly simple soul has extreme difficulty distinguishing between the good and the bad in anything or anyone; in fact, he anchors his own concept of Christianity to a blind faith in the nonexistent humaneness of his fellow creatures, an ideal he has gleaned from pursuing nonexistent principles. Totally lacking in experience, he possesses not the slightest idea of the actual composition of his society or the effects of its powerful but corruptive influences upon man. Nonetheless, Adams's conclusions about George

Whitefield exist (according to Fielding) as his most single, accurate statement; it stands, as it were, as his sole moment of truth; it places him on a parallel with the majority of rational eighteenth-century traditionalists. Therefore, if the likes of Abraham Adams can comprehend the evils of Methodism, to what pits of intellect must Whitefield and the Wesleys stoop to gain converts to their movement? For Henry Fielding, the question hardly demands an answer.

The dramatist Samuel Foote, although having nothing fresh to add to the thesis of anti-Methodism, does provide an additional perspective from which to view the argument. Foote earned a reputation not from his pen, but as a result of his talents at mimicry. Acting in his own plays, he could personally press home the ridicule that he heaped upon his fellow actors, leading personages of the day, and the various social, political, and theological institutions that seemed to threaten his own sense of reason and feel for tradition. Thus, in 1760, he wrote *The Minor*, a satire on the worn theme of the prodigal son, but boosted somewhat by a harsh assault upon George Whitefield and his Methodist colleagues. Mother Cole (usually played by Foote himself), the principal bawd of the piece, pretends to be a serious convert to Methodism, as she relies upon Whitefield's language and mannerisms to tempt the hero, young George Wealthy, into her palace of pleasure. For example, she describes her reformation as "a wonderful work! There had I been tossing in a sea of sin without rudder or compass; and had not the good gentleman piloted me into the harbour of grace, I must have struck against the rocks of reprobation, and have been quite swallowed up in the whirlpool of despair. He was the precious instrument of my spiritual sprinkling. —But, however, Sir George, if your mind be set upon a young country thing, to-morrow night, I believe, I can furnish you."[10]

Purely, Mother Cole's function, as well as that of Mr. Squintum (another model for Whitefield), who converted her, is to expose the absurdity and the hypocrisy of Methodism. If such as she could gain admittance to the fold, then the doors were open to anyone. A considerable number of London theater audiences must have agreed with the reasoning behind this attack upon Methodism, for Foote was still playing the part of Mother Cole at the Haymarket in August 1776, sixteen years after the play had first opened. According to one biographer of the playwright and actor, *The Minor* "seemed more effectually to open our eyes, those of the populace especially, in regard to the absurdities of that set of enthusiasts, than all the more serious writings that had been published against them."[11] Criticism and pressure from politicians, clerics, news-sheets, and influential Methodists had caused Foote to decrease somewhat the volume of his invective against Whitefield, but the dramatist's comic ridicule of Methodism continued to remain a favorite with the cultivated among the Establishment.

From the point of view of that Establishment, Methodism truly deserved such attacks as those described and illustrated throughout this chapter. Generally, John and Charles Wesley, George Whitefield, and Lady Huntingdon, together with their followers, were identified by Anglican loyalists as aliens operating against an essentially good world. The Methodists seemingly typified a fanatical element of society hovering around the fringe of tradition, whose mere presence prevented eighteenth-century Britain from achieving perfection in the eyes of God. The Establishment also viewed the Methodists as having inherited the principles of Protestant Dissent; they threatened (so it was thought) to reignite the same flames of conflict and chaos that had made life so difficult during the reigns of Charles II, James II, William and Mary, Anne, and the first George. Further, a significant proportion, headed by George Whitefield and kept aloft by the Countess of Huntingdon, were adherents of the philosophy of John Calvin; their enthusiasm brought out the old antagonisms against Calvinist doctrine: election, severity, pride, and antinomianism. Finally, the King and Church actually believed that Whitefield and the Wesleys led good and faithful Anglicans astray and threatened the stability guaranteed to the faithful by the Church of England.

Certainly the majority of the writers of mid- and late-eighteenth-century England interpreted Methodism in light of the above-mentioned antagonisms. They thus sought to direct their views outward for public consumption, for the instruction and entertainment of their audiences. In such a context, the cultivated men of letters had objectives similar to those of their less talented colleagues, the anti-Methodist pamphleteers and dissident Anglican clerics: to explore the various means by which Methodism could be neutralized; to smash its seemingly radical doctrines, disciplines, and institutions upon the bulwarks of the traditionalism and reason of the *via media*, the middle road that led directly to the nearest Anglican cathedral.

They hoped sensible persons would recognize the flaws in the new enthusiasm and turn their hearts and minds (especially their minds!) from it. Fortunately for Methodism, as a social force and as a religious ideal, and perhaps even fortunately for the entire kingdom, these writers, no matter what their levels of ability, never really came close to fulfilling their combined purpose.

The essential weakness of the anti-Methodist argument of the period is that it lacked real substance. The leaders of the movement, as well as the rank and file dedicated to its ideals, had never committed serious violations against Church, state, or king. Instead of statutes that might legally fine and convict Methodists, that might drive them to Newgate, Tyburn, or to the colonies, there existed only rocks, dead cats and dogs, cattle, and hired thugs—all functioning as mere accoutrements for harassment. Writers who had absolutely no idea how to go about stemming the influence of Methodism attempted to combat it with the only weapons at their disposal: ridicule, burlesque, sarcasm, and—when everything else failed—foul language and base metaphor. They succeeded principally in making people laugh, a purpose that was not hard to accomplish in the England of the eighteenth century. Moreover, the majority of the hacks and the *literati* found themselves preaching to the converted: Sterne, Smollett, and Fielding, for example, were practically foreign to Methodist eyes and minds, while the London stage of Samuel Foote ranked high on the list of John Wesley's social and intellectual heresies. Therefore, as with a number of other significant social and theological movements, Methodism stood firm in the path of rhetorical barrages that may have stung but did not destroy. Simply, the efforts of John and Charles Wesley were essential to the particular social conditions that gave rise to their mission; no amount of language, no skillful manipulations of tradition on the part of Britain's intellectuals, could bring about the elimination of Methodism or even seriously alter its direction. If anything, the majority of those who snatched up their pens and ran to attack Methodism succumbed, in the name of reason and in terms of their own concept of the enlightenment, to an enthusiasm far in excess of that which they had assaulted.

Notes and References

Chapter One

1. See Adam Clarke, *Memoirs of the Wesley Family* (London: J. and T. Clarke, 1823); Thomas Jackson, *Life of Charles Wesley* (London: Wesleyan Conference Office, 1841); J. C. Stevenson, *Memorials of the Wesley Family* (London: Methodist Conference Offices, 1876); E. B. Chappell, *Studies in the Life of John Wesley* (Nashville, Tenn., and London: South, Smith, and Lamar, 1911). Sir Leslie Stephen even included such information in his *DNB* entries on Samuel Wesley the elder and John and Charles Wesley. For more accurate information and assessment of the problem, see Charles Evans, "Ancestry of the Wesleys," *Notes and Queries* 193 (June 1948):255–59; and Elizabeth Langford, *Wellington: The Years of the Sword* (New York: Harper and Row, 1969), pp. 6–7.

2. Throughout the seventeenth century, the name was spelled WESTLEY.

3. A body of thirty-eight commissioners appointed by Cromwell to approve preachers and lecturers before their admissions to benefices.

4. The reader's attention is directed to the religious aspect of the Restoration settlement, known as the "Clarendon Code"—four statutes aimed not to tolerate religious dissent, but to destroy it.

5. Edward Everett, *Everett's Orations and Speeches* (1858), 3:306; quoted in S. A. Allibone, *Dictionary of English Literature* (Philadelphia: J. P. Lippincott, 1858), 3:2687.

6. In 1686, Charles Morton left England for Massachusetts, expecting to be named President of Harvard College. However, the appointment never materialized; on Friday, 5 November 1686, he was ordained minister of the church of Charlestown. He founded an academy intended to rival Harvard, but the officers of the college managed to close it. As compensation, Morton was elected a fellow of Harvard in 1692, and he rose to the vice presidency in 1692.

7. In his *DNB* article on John Dunton, Sir Leslie Stephen supposes that Samuel Wesley, Dunton, and Defoe all married daughters of Samuel Annesley. Defoe, however, married Mary Tuffley, who brought him a dowry of £3700 and then seven children.

8. From 5 through 15 February 1737, while at Savannah, John Wesley read Owen's *Display of Arminianisme* (London, 1642) to Sophia Hopkey,

presumably to reinforce, in both their minds, the duties and responsibilities of a clergyman.

9. Sources differ slightly on the specifics of Samuel Wesley's finances: Southey claims *(Life of Wesley)* that he entered Exeter with £2 16s. and left, in 1688, with £10 16s. John Telford (in his biographies of John and Charles Wesley) asserts with confidence that Wesley came to Oxford with £2 5s. and departed with £10, while during his entire term of residence, he received five shillings from family and friends.

10. As late as 1686, the registers of Exeter College show the spelling as WESTLEY (Southey, *Life of Wesley*, pp. 7–8, note 2). From this point on in the text, I use the spelling WESLEY.

11. Henry R. Plomer et al., *A Dictionary of Printers and Booksellers . . . 1688 to 1725* (London: Oxford University Press, 1922), p. 109.

12. John Telford *(Life of John Wesley*, p. 9) confidently claims that Samuel Wesley attended Dunton's wedding, although he offers no documentation.

13. The full title: *Maggots, or Poems on Several Subjects never before handled. To which is added, A pleasant account how many yards a nimble Louse reaches at hop, stride, and jump: Together with a Treatise of the Cause, Essence, and Properties of a piece of Gingerbread. Written by an Oxford Scholar. Octavo Printed for John Dunton at the Black Raven, at the corner of Prince's street; near the Royal Exchange.*

14. The original agreement among Dunton, Sault, and Wesley on 10 April 1691 is in the Rawlinson MSS. at the Bodleian.

15. Known as the "Old Pretender," James was born on 10 June 1688 at St. James's Palace, many believing that he was really introduced in a warming-pan.

16. H. N. Fairchild, *Religious Trends in English Poetry* (New York: Columbia University Press, 1939–1968), 1:113.

17. See John Butt, ed., *The Poems of Alexander Pope. A One-Volume Edition of the Twickenham Text* (New Haven: Yale University Press, 1963), p. 360, and my essay "Pope and the Wesleys," *University of Dayton Review* 9 (1972):47–57. Earlier in the same book of *The Dunciad Variorum* (1729), Pope had referred to "Maggots half-form'd, in rhyme exactly meet, / And learn to crawl upon poetic feet" (ll. 59–60, p. 354).

18. Jonathan Swift, *Gulliver's Travels and Other Writings* (Boston: Houghton Mifflin Co., 1960), p. 373.

19. George Sherburn, ed., *The Correspondence of Alexander Pope* (Oxford: Clarendon Press, 1956), 3:104–5.

20. See Elwin and Courthope, eds., *The Works of Alexander Pope* (1871–1889; reprint ed., New York, 1967), 7:193, 197.

21. Clarke, *Memoirs of the Wesley Family*, 1:330, and John Telford, ed., *The Letters of John Wesley* (London: Epworth Press, 1931), 1:192.

22. In Samuel Wesley's time, Epworth was a market town of approximately 2,000 people, the principal place in the Isle of Axholme, a strip of land formerly enclosed by five rivers: Idle, Torr (west and south), Trent (east), Ouse, Don, Humber estuary (north). For a description of the area and the rectory at Epworth, see Telford's *Life of Charles Wesley* (pp. 12–13) and his *Life of John Wesley* (pp. 11–13).

23. Southey, *Life of Wesley*, p. 8.

24. Nehemiah Curnock, ed., *The Journal of John Wesley* (London, 1909–1916), 3:36. John Wesley inserted into his journal for 1 August 1742, the day of Susanna Wesley's burial in Bunhill Fields, London, two letters written by his mother. The first is to her husband (6 February 1712), the second is the one from which I have cited. Both refer to the education of her children.

25. *Journal*, 3:38–39.

26. *Journal*, 3:33. Those of us who keep track of numbers will notice that two children are missing from the list—Samuel the younger and Keziah. The former was then at Oxford, while the latter was not yet two years old when the letter was written.

Chapter Two

1. Joan. Westley as nominat. ducis de Bucks admiss. in fundat. Carthus. 28 Jan. 1713/14—ad Univ. 24 June, 1720. *Journal*, 1:465–66. The Latin quotation is from a memorandum in Wesley's own handwriting.

2. Telford, *Life of John Wesley*, p. 23.

3. The latter group wore broadcloth gowns lined with coarse wool (or baize) and were known as "gown-boys."

4. Thomas Burnet, *Telluris Theoria Sacra* (London, 1681 and 1689).

5. Luke Tyerman, *Life of Wesley* (1870; reprint ed., New York, 1872), 1:22.

6. Wesley's *Letters* (ed. Telford), 1:5.

7. George Stanhope (1660–1728), Dean of Canterbury, translated the *Imitatione Christi* in 1696; several editions of that translation followed.

8. Wesley was the eleventh and most junior Fellow of Lincoln College. At his appointment, Dr. John Morley served as rector, while John Brereton was senior Fellow and subrector. Each fellow was expected to proceed to the Bachelor of Divinity Degree and then to complete, within seven years, the degree of Master of Arts. Wesley never bothered with the first responsibility and thus remained, until he resigned in 1751, the most junior Fellow. The resignation was caused by his marriage, since only bachelors could be appointed to and hold fellowships. No doubt Wesley saw certain advantages in an association with Oxford (as with the Church of England), and therefore held on to his fellowship for as long as he possibly could.

9. Telford, *Life of Wesley*, p. 49.

10. *Journal*, 6:110.

11. Quoted in Telford's *Life of Charles Wesley*, p. 33.

12. *Arminian Magazine* 7 (1784):387.

13. Southey, *Life of Wesley*, p. 31.

14. For Wesley's own view of Oxford Methodism, see his letter to Richard Morgan, William Morgan's father, of 18 October 1732 *(Letters,* 1:121–33).

15. The Holy Club never had a large membership—never exceeding fourteen between 1732 and 1735.

Chapter Three

1. The intention in this chapter, as in those that follow, is to focus upon the literary strengths of the Wesleys and merely to gloss over those areas that are secondary or repetitive. Although Charles Wesley maintained diaries and journals and wrote letters and sermons, the material contained in those works tends to echo the thoughts and the activities of his elder brother. In Chapter 4, the reverse will hold true, and thus there is no real need to discuss the details of a relatively few pieces of poetry written by John Wesley.

2. James Boswell, *Life of Johnson* (London: Oxford University Press, 1970), p. 898.

3. *Journal*, 1:83.

4. Both Wesley's sources and the actual cipher are not to be confused with those of Samuel Pepys. The latter relied exclusively on *A Tutor to Tachygraphy, or Short-Writing* (London: Samuel Cartwright, 1642) and *Tachygraphy. The Most Exact and Compendious Methode of Short and Swift Writing* (Cambridge: Roger Daniel, 1647). Both have been reprinted— Los Angeles: The Augustan Reprint Society, 1970, publication numbers 145–146.

5. *Journal*, 7:525.

6. *Journal*, 1:111.

7. *Journal*, 1:109.

8. Epaminondas of Thebes defeated the invading Spartans at Leuctra.

9. In his *Thoughts concerning Religion*, John Hutchinson affirmed that the Scriptures contained the elements not only of true religion, but of all rational philosophy. "I shall never receive Mr. Hutchinson's creed," maintained John Wesley, "unless *ipse dixit* pass for evidence" *(Journal*, 4:190).

10. The play was produced in 1739 and prohibited the same year under the Licensing Act of 21 June 1737, although it is difficult to uncover any political or satirical material that would have offended the Walpole ministry.

11. In his *Life of Thomson*, Johnson writes, "His diction is in the highest degree florid and luxuriant, such as may be said to be his images and thoughts 'both their lustre and their shade'; such as invest them with

splendour, through which perhaps they are not always easily discerned" (*Lives of the . . . English Poets*, ed. Peter Cunningham [London: John Murray, 1854], 3:240).

12. William Law was a disciple of Jakob Boehme, the German mystic. For Boehme, God was original and undistinguished unity, at once everything and nothing, through which everything comes into existence. He explained creation through the principle of negation, which he identified with evil. See Wesley's *Thoughts upon Jacob Behmen* (1780).

13. The three quotations in this paragraph are from Shakespeare's *Julius Caesar* (3:2:195), Milton's *Paradise Lost* (11:269), and Pope's *Epitaph. On Mrs. Corbet, Who dyed of a Cancer in her Breast* (ll. 7–10).

14. From Propertius's compliment to Virgil in reference to the latter's *Aeneid*: "Your places yield, ye bards of Greece and Rome; / A greater than the Iliad is come."

15. The original reads, "A little rule. . . ."

16. William Tytler, *An Historical and Critical Inquiry into the Evidence . . . against Mary, Queen of Scots* (Edinburgh, 1760).

17. Wentworth House, in Yorkshire, seat of the Marquis of Rockingham. Obviously, Wesley was not, as evidenced by the quick generalization in the middle of this passage, impressed by the art of Van Dyck, several of whose paintings were hanging in Wentworth House.

18. To Simon Day, from Newcastle, 1 June 1784. This is Wesley's shortest letter, appointing Day a preacher in the Oxfordshire circuit. See *Letters*, ed. Telford, 3:219 (all references are to this edition, unless otherwise indicated).

19. See, especially, *Journal*, 1:181–82; Tyerman, *Life of John Wesley*, 1:143–46; Arnold Lunn, *John Wesley* (New York, 1929), pp. 66–82.

20. See *Journal*, 3:513–17, for additional details. The circumstances leading to Wesley's marriage, as well as the opposition to the event (particularly from brother Charles), are too entangled for discussion here. A summary of events appears in my essay "John Wesley's Women," *Eighteenth-Century Life* 1 (October 1974):9–10.

21. *Journal*, 6:337.

22. "Therefore (or such) I am: If you love me, use me." See *Letters*, 4:215.

Chapter Four

1. *Charlestown* [Charleston, South Carolina]: *Timothy, 1737—the first hymn book to be issued in America* (reprint ed., London: William Strahan, 1739).

2. Henry Bett, *The Hymns of Methodism*, 3rd ed. (London, 1945), pp. 21–32.

3. As late as 1962, over 1,300 poems by Charles Wesley remained unpublished. See Frank Baker, *Representative Verse of Charles Wesley* (London: Epworth Press, 1962).

4. George Osborn, ed., *The Poetical Works of John and Charles Wesley* (London: Wesleyan Methodist Conference Office, 1868–1872), 6:181; all references to this edition, unless otherwise indicated.

5. Johnson, *Lives of the Poets*, ed. Cunningham, 2:207.

6. Donald Greene, *The Age of Exuberance: Background to Eighteenth-Century English Literature* (New York: Random House, 1970), p. 83.

7. See Telford, *Life of Charles Wesley*, pp. 207–15, 238–46, 308–9; Hoxie Neale Fairchild, *Religious Trends in English Poetry* (New York: Columbia University Press, 1939–1968), 2:80–81, 91.

8. John Wesley's *Explanatory Notes on the New Testament* appeared in 1755; Robert Gell wrote *Essays towards the Amendment of the English Translation of the Bible* (London, 1659) and *Remains, or Select Scriptures of the New Testament* (2 vols., London, 1676); the Welsh Nonconformist Matthew Henry published a five-volume *Commentary on the Holy Scriptures* (London, 1708–1710) and *An Exposition of the Prophetical Books of the Old Testament* (1712); the exegetical commentary by J. A. Bengel, *Gnomon Novi Testamenti*, appeared in 1742.

9. Actually, by the time of Charles Wesley's death in 1788, the number of hymn paraphrases of Scriptures had increased to 5,100—1,609 from the Old Testament and 3,491 from the New Testament.

10. All biblical citations are from the King James Version.

11. Erik Routley, *The Musical Wesleys* (London, 1968), p. 31.

12. *A Collection of Hymns for the use of the People called Methodists* (London: Printed for J. Paramore, at the Foundery, 1780). From the "Preface," dated 20 October 1779. The hymnal was issued in conjunction with the opening of the new Chapel at City Road, London.

Chapter Five

1. From 14 January 1747 through 25 December 1761, John Wesley maintained a sermon register, a summary of his pulpit activity arranged in three columns: date, place, and the biblical text upon which the sermon was based.

2. During fall and winter 1738–1739, the Bishop of London banned Wesley from preaching in practically every Anglican church in London. Allhallows was no exception. Officials of the church on Lombard Street were the first to allow him to return, on 28 January 1776.

3. *Journal*, 6:96; *Wesleyan Methodist Magazine*, 3d ser., no. 4 (1825):105; Tyerman's *Life of Wesley*, 3:563.

4. John Wesley, *Sermons on Several Occasions*, ed. Thomas Jackson (1825; reprint ed., New York: Carlton and Phillips, 1854), 1:6; all references to this edition, unless otherwise indicated.

5. *Journal*, 5:396–397.

6. *Journal*, 6:83. Wesley wrote his text in London on Sunday, 5 November 1775.

7. *Letters*, 6:83, 155–60, 160–64 contain the pleas to Lords Dartmouth and North against sending troops to America. See *Journal*, 6:66–70; 8:325–28; and my essay "John Wesley on War and Peace," in *Studies in Eighteenth-Century Culture* (Madison: University of Wisconsin Press, 1978), pp. 329–44.

8. *PW*, 8:335.

9. In *The Works of John Wesley*, ed. Gerald R. Cragg (Oxford: Oxford University Press, 1975), 2:49; all references to the *Appeals* from this edition.

10. Following the seventy-eighth word. The paragraph contains 152 words; there are five direct quotations totaling thirty-three words (or 23 percent of the total number of words in the paragraph).

11. There are 165 words, three quotations, and forty quoted words comprising 24 percent of the total.

12. Interestingly, 50 of the 101 paragraphs of *An Earnest Appeal* end with direct quotations.

13. The quotation, "guiding . . . peace" is from Luke 1:79.

14. Taylor wrote the work in 1735.

15. Clarence H. Faust and Thomas H. Johnson, eds., *Jonathan Edwards*, rev. ed. (New York: Hill and Wang, 1962), pp. lxvi–lxxiv.

16. *Letters*, 4:48.

17. *Letters*, 4:67.

18. *Journal*, 3:520.

19. Thomas Jackson, ed., *The Works of the Rev. John Wesley* (1829–1831; reprint ed., Grant Rapids, Michigan, 1958–1959), 9:192, 193, 193–94. Unless otherwise indicated, all references to Wesley's prose tracts from this edition, hereafter cited as *Works*.

20. Jacobus Arminius (1560–1609), a Dutch Reformed theologian, after careful study of Paul's epistle to the Romans, doubted the Calvinistic doctrine of predestination.

21. *Letters*, 7:27–28. Taylor was sixty-seven when he died; Wesley was seventy-seven in August 1780.

22. *Brief Thoughts on Christian Perfection* (27 January 1767), in *Works*, 11:446.

23. The text in the Jackson edition (vol. 11) of the *Works* goes forward to 1777; all references to Wesley's *Plain Account* in my text are from that edition.

Chapter Six

1. *Journal*, 5:523.

2. *Journal*, 5:458.

3. *Journal*, 5:491. Samuel Johnson expressed negative reactions to Dalrymple; he thought the historian's style to be "the mere bouncing of a schoolboy. Great He! but greater She! and such stuff." On another occasion, he accused him of foppery (Boswell's *Life*, ed. R. W. Chapman and J. D. Fleeman [London: Oxford University Press, 1970.], pp. 508, 527).

4. *Letters*, 5:199.

5. Samuel Clarke.

6. *Journal*, 6:63.

7. *Journal*, 6:22–23.

8. *Journal*, 6:326.

9. *Ibid.* John Toland (1670–1722), the Irish deistical writer, published *Nazarenus* in 1718.

10. John Hawkesworth (1715–1773), editor of the *Adventurer* and of Swift's works, and author of an *Account of the Voyage of Byron, Wallis, Cartaret, and Cook*, 3 vols. (London, 1773).

11. *Journal*, 6:326.

12. *Works*, 11:275.

13. Joseph Benson (1749–1821), like Fletcher, was one of John Wesley's most devoted followers. After Wesley's death, he rose to a position of leadership within the Conference.

14. *Works*, 13:418.

15. Spence, friend of Pope and professor of poetry at Oxford, 1728–1738, collected anecdotes on literary figures of the day; although the anecdotes remained in manuscript until 1820, they were available (though not made public) to certain examiners. Johnson, for instance, consulted them for his *Lives of the Poets*.

16. Bett, *Hymns of Methodism*, pp. 156–60. That influence continued throughout the Wesleys' careers. John included the complete text of *Henry and Emma* in the *Arminian Magazine* for 1779; it consumed fourteen pages, and functioned, perhaps, as a form of passive resistance to Johnson's *Life of Prior*, also 1779. The readers of the *Magazine*, however, objected to the poem on the grounds that it was not strictly religious and was thus out of place in an obviously religious journal. As usual, Wesley had the last word, maintaining that those who "read it without tears must have a stupid and unfeeling heart" (Tyerman, *Life of Wesley*, 3:317).

17. Samuel Johnson, "Prior," in *Lives of the English Poets*, ed. G. B. Hill (Oxford: Oxford University Press, 1905), 2:202. Italics in this and in the quotations immediately following are mine.

18. Matthew Prior, "Solomon on the Vanity of the World. A Poem in Three Books," in *The Literary Works of Matthew Prior*, ed. H. B. Wright and M. K. Spears (Oxford: Oxford University Press, 1959), 1:329.

19. Alexander Pope, "Elegy to the Memory of an Unfortunate Lady," in John Butt, ed., *The Poems of Alexander Pope* (New Haven: Yale University Press, 1963), p. 262.

20. Boswell, *Life of Johnson*, pp. 900, 951, 324–25.

21. *Journal*, 6:466.

22. Quite possibly, Wesley even owed Johnson a debt for his copy of the *Life of Prior*. In 1959, the Pierpont Morgan Library exhibited a set of the 1781 edition of the *Lives of the Poets* supposedly presented by Johnson to Wesley. See R. E. Brantley, "Johnson's Wesleyan Connection," *ECS* 10 (Winter 1976/1977):148.

Chapter Seven

1. *Works*, 13:474. Rousseau published *Emile*, in which he presented his views on education, in 1762.

2. *Works*, 14:217.

3. *Works*, 14:233.

4. *Works*, 13:291.

5. *Works*, 14:4–5.

6. *PW*, 6:432.

7. Again, these were the same hymns published by Charles Wesley in 1763.

Chapter Eight

1. *Works*, 11:15.

2. Because of his attacks upon the Revolution Settlement and the Act of Toleration, the House of Lords impeached Henry Sacheverell in 1710, found him guilty, and prohibited him from preaching for three years. His troubles came to an end, however, when the Godolphin ministry fell in 1710; in 1713 the House of Commons selected him to preach the Restoration sermon.

3. Francesco Cordasco, *A Junius Bibliography*, rev. ed. (New York: Burt Franklin, 1949), pp. 10, 22–28.

4. John Hampson, *Memoirs of the Late John Wesley* (Sunderland: J. Graham, 1791), 3:160. Other than Hampson, neither the quotation nor the offer has been uncovered.

5. *Works*, 11:34.

6. The Thirty-nine Articles constitute the doctrinal formulas finally accepted by the Church of England. The Convocation of 1563 issued the initial text, and it was put into final form in 1571. The Articles are not to be considered a creed of Christian doctrine, but serve as short summaries

of dogmatic tenets, each concerned with a point raised in contemporary controversy. Prior to 1865, Anglican clergy were required to subscribe totally to the Articles; afterward, only an affirmation of general assent became necessary.

7. *Journal*, 5:445–46.

8. Charles Stuart, *A Memoir of Granville Sharpe* (1836; reprint ed., Westport, Conn.: Negro Universities Press, 1970), p. 13. Sharpe (1735–1813) served as the first chairman of the London committee for the abolition of the British slave trade, organized in the spring of 1787.

9. Quoted in Stuart, *Memoirs*, p. 21.

10. *Works*, 11:59.

11. In 1813, the British government purchased Hargrave's law library for £8000 and placed the volumes in the British Museum.

12. *Journal*, 11:66–67, note 3.

13. *The Works of Samuel Johnson, LL.D.* (1825; reprint ed., New York, 1970), 6:236.

14. *Works*, 11:86–88.

15. *Works of Samuel Johnson*, 6:257.

16. W. E. H. Lecky, *England in the Eighteenth Century* (London: Longmans, Green, 1883–1890), 3:530.

17. Richard Price, *Additional Observations on the Nature and Value of Civil Liberty and the War with America* (London: 1777) and *The General Introduction and Supplement to the Two Tracts on Civil Liberty, the War with America, and the Finances of the Kingdom* (London: 1778).

18. *Journal*, 6:100.

19. *Works*, 11:94.

20. John Wesley, *A Calm Address to the Inhabitants of England* (London: J. Fry and Co., 1777), pp. 3–4; all references to this edition.

21. Oliver Goldsmith, *History of England* (London, 1764); Paul de Rapin, *Histoire d'Angleterre* (1724); Tobias Smollett, *History of England* (London, 1756).

22. *Journal*, 6:96, note 1.

23. *Journal*, 3:301.

24. *Letters*, 6:200.

25. John Wesley, *Primitive Physick* (1747; reprint ed., Santa Barbara, Calif.: Woodbridge Press, 1975), p. 10; all references to this edition.

26. A 1975 reprint of *Primitive Physick* contains the following publisher's note: "This authentic reproduction . . . is presented as a work of cultural and entertainment interest only. Wesley's philosophy of natural good health certainly provides a valid basis for preventive health care and many of these suggested remedies are as valid today as they were two hundred years ago. Nevertheless, the reader should consider them in light

of contemporary health knowledge and confer with his physician or other health counsellor in using them."

27. Charles F. Mullett, ed., *The Letters of Dr. George Cheyne to Samuel Richardson (1733–1743)* (Columbia, Mo.: University of Missouri Press, 1943), p. 49.

28. *Journal*, 6:53–54.

29. *Letters*, 4:121.

30. J. H. Plumb, *England in the Eighteenth Century* (Harmondsworth, England: Penguin, 1963), p. 96.

Chapter Nine

1. S. P. Cadman, *The Three Religious Leaders of Oxford and Their Movements* (New York: Macmillan, 1916), p. 38.

2. Evan Lloyd, *The Methodist* (1766; reprint ed., Los Angeles: Augustan Reprint Society, 1962), p. 13; all references are to this edition.

3. Boswell, *Journal of a Tour to the Hebrides*, ed. R. W. Chapman (London: Oxford University Press, 1930), p. 425.

4. Boswell, *Life of Johnson*, ed. Chapman-Fleeman, p. 409.

5. Boswell, *Life of Johnson*, pp. 324–25.

6. Laurence Sterne, *Tristram Shandy*, ed. Ian Watt (Boston: Houghton Mifflin, 1965), p. 172.

7. Tobias Smollett, *Humphry Clinker*, ed. Andre Parreaux (Boston: Houghton Mifflin, 1968), p. 127.

8. *Journal*, 6:229–230. Why would he be "surprised," since he had relied upon the *Complete History* as a source for his own *Concise History of England* (see Chapter 9)? Obviously, Wesley has gotten around to reading a different edition from the one he had consulted in 1775–1776.

9. Henry Fielding, *Joseph Andrews*, ed. Maynard Mack (New York: Holt, Rinehart, 1948), pp. 67–68.

10. Samuel Foote, *Dramatic Works* (1809; reprint ed., New York: Burt Franklin, n.d.), 1:33.

11. *Dramatic Works*, 1:12.

Selected Bibliography

This list focuses upon sources emphasizing John and Charles Wesley as men of letters. For more extensive bibliographic information, particularly on eighteenth-century Methodism and the Wesleys' theology, see the entries below under Bibliography.

PRIMARY SOURCES

1. Bibliography

Baker, Frank. *Union Catalogue of the Publications of John and Charles Wesley*. Durham, N.C.: Duke University, 1966. A locating bibliography for all of the major and several minor collections of the brothers' prose and poetry.

A Catalogue of Wesleyana. London: Sharp, 1921. Lists the manuscripts, relics, engravings, photographs, books, medals, pamphlets, pottery, and medallions belonging to the Wesleyan Methodist Conference, London.

Catalogue of Wesleyana in the Library of Queen's College, University of Melbourne. Melbourne, Australia: University of Melbourne, 1926.

Green, Richard. *The Works of John and Charles Wesley*. 2d ed. London: Charles H. Kelly, 1896. The first systematic bibliography; the works appear in chronological order, transcribing the title-pages of first editions and listing other editions. Contains 417 works, 283 of them original. Not always reliable.

Jones, Arthur, and Kline, Lawrence. *Union Checklist of Editions of the Publications of John and Charles Wesley*. Madison, N.J.: Drew University, 1960. The basis for Baker's *Catalogue*; prepared for the Methodist Librarians' Fellowship.

Norwood, Frederick A. "Methodist Historical Studies, 1930–1959." *Church History* 28 (1959):391, 417; 29 (1960):74–88. Bibliographical and historical materials on the Wesleys and British and American Methodism.

————. "Wesleyan and Methodist Historical Studies, 1960–1970." *Church History* 40 (June 1971):182–89. A continuation of the earlier essays.

Osborn, George. *Outlines of Wesleyan Bibliography*. London: Wesleyan Conference Office, 1869. The standard bibliography prior to Green. Lists works of the Wesleys and selected eighteenth- and nineteenth-century Methodists.

Rogal, Samuel J. "The Wesleys. A Checklist of Critical Commentary." *Bulletin of Bibliography* 28 (January-March 1971):22–35. Entries arranged under subject headings; journals coded in entries but listed separately in an appendix.

Swift, Wesley F. A "Bibliographical Study of Wesley's *Works*." *Proceedings of the Wesley Historical Society* 31 (1951):173–77. Concerns the various editions of John Wesley's collected works.

2. Charles Wesley

The Journal of the Rev. Charles Wesley, M.A. Edited by Thomas Jackson. 2 vols. London: Mason, 1849.

The Journal of the Rev. Charles Wesley: The Early Journal, 1736–1739. Edited by John. London: Culley, 1909.

Sermons by the Late Rev. Charles Wesley. London: Baldwin, Cradock, and Joy, 1816.

The Poetical Works of John and Charles Wesley. Edited by George Osborn. 13 vols. London: Wesleyan Methodist Conference Office, 1868–1872.

Representative Verse of Charles Wesley. Selected and Edited with an Introduction by Frank Baker. London: Epworth Press, 1963.

3. John Wesley

The Works of the Rev. John Wesley. 32 vols. Bristol: William Pine, 1771–1774.

The Works of John Wesley. Edited by Joseph Benson. 17 vols. London: Wesleyan Conference Office, 1809–1813.

The Works of the Rev. John Wesley. Edited by Thomas Jackson. 14 vols. London: Wesleyan Conference Office, 1829–1831.

The Oxford Edition of the Works of John Wesley. Edited by Frank Baker et al. 34 vols. (proposed). Oxford: At the Clarendon Press, 1975—.

The Journal of the Rev. John Wesley, A.M. Edited by Nehemiah Curnock. 8 vols. London: Charles H. Kelly, 1909–1916.

The Letters of the Rev. John Wesley, A.M. Edited by John Telford. 8 vols. London: Epworth Press, 1931.

The Standard Sermons of John Wesley. Edited by Edward H. Sugden. 2 vols. London: Epworth Press, 1921.

SECONDARY SOURCES

·1. The Wesleys
A. Books
Clarke, Adam. *Memoirs of the Wesley Family.* 2 vols. London: J. and T. Clarke, 1823. Contains a considerable amount of information, but the reader must be careful to distinguish between fact and anecdote.
Crook, William. *The Ancestry of the Wesleys, with Special Reference to Their Connexion with Ireland.* London: Epworth Press, 1938.
Edwards, Maldwyn L. *Sons to Samuel.* London: Epworth Press, 1961. Valuable for its treatment of life at Epworth, the relationship between Samuel and Susanna Wesley, and the education of the Wesleys.
Harmon, Rebecca Lamar. *Susanna, Mother of the Wesleys.* Nashville: Abingdon Press, 1968. Discusses the education of the Epworth Wesleys, with emphasis upon their mother's strong character and influence.
Newton, John Anthony. *Susanna Wesley and the Puritan Tradition in Methodism.* London: Epworth Press, 1968. Interprets the Wesleys' mother in terms of her Puritan background and influences.
Routley, Erik. *The Musical Wesleys.* London: Herbert Jenkins, 1968. Although the emphasis is upon Charles Wesley's sons, there is sufficient discussion of the musical influence of John and Charles and the role of music within the evangelical revival of the eighteenth century.
Stevenson, George J. *Memorials of the Wesley Family.* London: Methodist Conference Office, 1876. More reliable than the effort of Adam Clarke.
Tyerman, Luke. *Life and Times of Samuel Wesley.* London: Simpkin, Marshall and Co., 1866. Concerns Samuel Wesley the elder. Despite its date and Tyerman's Methodist fervor, the work is still valid, principally because the students of the Epworth rector have little else from which to choose.
Vallins, George H. *The Wesleys and the English Language. Four Essays.* London: Epworth Press, 1957. Discusses the grammars and the *Dictionary*.

B. Articles
Baker, Frank. "Jonathan Swift and the Wesleys." *London Quarterly and Holborn Review* 179 (October 1954):290–300.
Beecham, H. A. "Samuel Wesley Senior. New Biographical Evidence." *Renaissance and Modern Studies* 7 (1963):78–109.
Evans, Charles. "Ancestry of the Wesleys." *Notes and Queries* 193 (June 1948):255–59.
Overton, John Henry. "Samuel Wesley and His Family at Epworth." *Longman's Magazine* 8 (1886):41.
Rogal, Samuel J. "Pope and the Wesleys." *University of Dayton Review* 9 (1972):47–57.

Sudgen, Edward H. "Samuel Wesley's Notes on Shakespeare." *London Quarterly Review* 139 (April 1923):157–72.

2. Charles Wesley

A. Books

Baker, Frank. *Charles Wesley: As Revealed by His Letters*. London: Epworth Press, 1948. Identifies the various difficulties in trying to construct an argument from primary sources, especially Charles Wesley's letters. Contains excerpts from about 600 letters.

————. *Charles Wesley's Verse: An Introduction*. London: Epworth Press, 1964. The best piece of critical commentary devoted to Charles Wesley's poetry. Written by a principal scholar on the Wesleys and eighteenth-century Methodism.

Bett, Henry. *The Hymns of Methodism*. 3d ed. London: The Epworth Press, 1945. Particularly valuable for concrete and detailed discussion of the influence of specific poets (classical and contemporary) upon the poetry of Charles Wesley.

Flew, Robert Newton. *The Hymns of Charles Wesley: A Study of Their Structure*. London: Epworth Press, 1953. The author seeks to apply the hymns to the theological needs of common man.

Gill, Frederick Cyril. *Charles Wesley, the First Methodist*. New York and Nashville: Abingdon Press, 1964. The best study of Charles Wesley, even though it is generally undocumented.

Haas, Alfred Burton. *Charles Wesley*. New York: Hymn Society of America, 1957. A monograph that surveys Charles Wesley's hymns.

Jackson, Thomas. *Life of Charles Wesley*. 2 vols. London: Wesleyan Conference Office, 1841. A carefully prepared, thorough project, referred to as the best Methodist history-biography until superseded by Tyerman and Telford.

Manning, Bernard Lord. *The Hymns of Wesley and Watts*. London: Epworth Press, 1942. Five lectures delivered between 1924 and 1939, all focusing on Charles Wesley, Isaac Watts, Methodist hymn books, and the religious elements in Charles Wesley's poetry.

Telford, John. *The Life of the Rev. Charles Wesley, M.A.* London: Methodist Book Room, 1900. A clearly written, thorough account based principally upon Wesley's journal, his letters, and Jackson's biography.

Wiseman, F. Luke. *Charles Wesley*. New York: Abingdon Press, 1932. A valuable, general biographical study, but hard to follow because events are not always in clear chronological order.

B. Articles

Beckerlegge, Oliver A. "An Attempt at a Classification of Charles Wesley's Metres: A Contribution to the Study of English Prosody." *London Quarterly and Holborn Review* 169 (July 1944):219–27.

————. "Charles Wesley's Vocabulary." *London Quarterly and Holborn Review* 193 (April 1968):152–61.

England, Martha Winburn. "Blake and the Hymns of Charles Wesley." *Bulletin of the New York Public Library* 70 (1966):7–26, 93–112, 153–68, 251–64.

————. "The First Wesley Hymn Book." *Bulletin of the New York Public Library* 68 (1964):225–38.

Findlay, George H. "First and Last Words: A Study of Some Wesley Metres." *London Quarterly and Holborn Review* 177 (April 1952):123–28.

————. "A Study in Wesley Six-Eighths." *London Quarterly and Holborn Review* 180 (1955):138–42.

Noll, Mark A. "Romanticism and the Hymns of Charles Wesley." *Evangelical Quarterly* 46 (1974):195–223.

Rogal, Samuel J. "The Occasional Hymns of Charles Wesley." *Cresset* 42 (January 1979):8–13.

Schelp, Hanspeter. "Wordsworth's 'Daffodils' Influenced by a Wesleyan Hymn." *English Studies* 42 (1961):307–9. Concerns Wesley's "When quiet in my house I sit."

C. Dissertations

Morris, Gilbert L. "Imagery in the Hymns of Charles Wesley." *DAI* 30 (1970):3018A (Arkansas).

Roth, Herbert John. "A Literary Study of the Calvinistic and Deistic Implications in the Hymns of Isaac Watts, Charles Wesley, and William Cowper." *DAI* 39 (1978):3604A–3605A.

Welch, Barbara A. "Charles Wesley and the Celebrations of Evangelical Experience." *DAI* 32 (1972):6461A–6462A (Michigan).

3. John Wesley

A. Books

Branburn, Samuel. *A Farther Account of the Reverend John Wesley.* Manchester, 1792. Written quickly after Wesley's death by a close friend of both Wesleys.

Cell, George Croft. *The Rediscovery of John Wesley.* New York: Holt, 1935. A reexamination of Wesley's religious principles in light of Calvinistic influences.

Coke, Thomas and More, Henry. *The Life of the Rev. John Wesley.* London: Methodist Conference Office, 1792. Relies on primary materials, but written hastily after Wesley's death, in an attempt to take advantage of the emotions of the moment.

Dobree, Bonamy. *Wesley.* London: Duckworth, 1933. A brief account emphasizing the earlier years.

Gill, Frederick Cyril. *In the Steps of John Wesley.* New York: Abingdon Press, 1964. A "geographical" biography that discusses Wesley within the context of the places where he visited and worked.

Green, J. Brazier. *John Wesley and William Law.* London: Epworth Press, 1945. Focuses upon the theological aspects of the two men, especially upon their literary efforts.

Green, Vivian Hubert Howard. *John Wesley.* London: Nelson, 1964. A solid, general survey of Wesley's life and times.

————. *The Young Mr. Wesley: A Study of John Wesley and Oxford.* New York: St. Martin's Press, 1961. Based largely upon the diaries for 1725–1735; presents some new, unpublished material.

Hampson, John. *Memoirs of the Late John Wesley.* 3 vols. Sunderland: J. Graham, 1791. A history of British Methodism between 1729 and 1790, and a review of Wesley's life and writings by an ambitious Methodist preacher who never forgave Wesley for excluding him from the inner circle of decision-making at the annual conferences.

Harrison, G. Elsie. *Haworth Parsonage: A Study of Wesley and the Brontës.* London: Epworth Press, 1937. Discusses early Methodism in Yorkshire, as well as Wesley's connections with the Brontës and his influence on certain aspects of their fiction.

————. *Son to Susanna. The Private Life of John Wesley.* London: Ivor Nicholson and Watson, 1937. Belongs to the "emotional" school of Wesleyan scholarship, but valuable for its insights into the Epworth daughters and Mrs. Vazielle.

Herbert, Thomas Walter. *John Wesley As Editor and Author.* Princeton: Princeton University Press, 1940. A scholarly discussion of Wesley's methods of abstracting, abridging, and editing.

Hill, Alfred Wesley. *John Wesley among the Physicians: A Study of Eighteenth-Century Medicine.* London: Epworth Press, 1958. Concludes that Wesley was not an amateur in matters of personal health and medical and scientific knowledge.

Hutton, William Holden. *The Life of John Wesley.* London: Macmillan, 1927. Briefly but systematically stresses the traits that allowed Wesley to become the leader of British Methodism.

Laver, James. *Wesley.* London: Davies, 1932. A brief (169 pp.) and highly subjective account of Wesley's personal life and religious development.

Lawton, George. *John Wesley's English: A Study of His Literary Style.* London: George Allen and Unwin, 1962.

Lee, Umphrey. *The Lord's Horseman: John Wesley the Man.* London: Hodder and Stoughton, 1956. An extremely sympathetic biography that views Wesley as his contemporaries supposedly saw and reacted to him.

Lipsky, Abram. *John Wesley: A Portrait.* New York: Simon and Schuster, 1928. Not only a biography, but a series of valuable discussions of

Wesley's sermons, revisions of hymns and poems, and prose style. Further, the reader views Wesley from psychological and social perspectives.

Lunn, Arnold Henry Moore. *John Wesley.* New York: Dial Press, 1929. Not a scholarly biography, yet treats Wesley with some degree of objectivity. Relies heavily upon the diaries and journals.

Marshall, Dorothy. *John Wesley.* London: Oxford University Press, 1965.

McConnell, Francis J. *John Wesley.* New York: Abingdon Press, 1939. A fairly objective study by a Methodist bishop who compares and contrasts facts from earlier biographies to separate points of view and identify errors.

Mitchell, T. Crichton. *Mr. Wesley: An Intimate Sketch of John Wesley.* Boston: Beacon Press, 1957.

Monk, Robert Clarence. *John Wesley: His Puritan Heritage.* Nashville: Abingdon Press, 1966. Focuses upon the similarities between Wesley and the Puritans, particularly in relation to the gospel and to daily life.

Nottingham, Elizabeth Kristine. *The Making of an Evangelist: A Study of John Wesley's Early Years.* Upper Darby, Pa.: C. S. McIver, 1938. A sociological treatment that focuses upon Wesley's social inheritance as it relates to life at Epworth, education at Oxford, and the mission to Georgia.

Rowe, Kenneth, ed. *The Place of Wesley in the Christian Tradition: Essays Delivered at Drew University in Celebration of the Commencement of the Publication of the Oxford Edition of the Works of John Wesley.* Metuchen, N.J.: Scarecrow Press, 1976.

Schmidt, Martin. *John Wesley: A Theological Biography.* Translated by Norman P. Goldhawk. Volume 1. London: Epworth Press, 1962; New York: Abingdon Press, 1962. Covers the period 17 June 1703 through May 1738—from Wesley's birth through the Aldersgate experience. From the German.

―――. *John Wesley: A Theological Biography.* Translated by Norman P. Goldhawk and Denis Inman. Volume 2. Nashville and New York: Abingdon Press, 1972–1973. Focuses upon Wesley as founder, organizer, administrator, and leader of British Methodism—his activities and the opposition he faced. From the German.

Southey, Robert. *The Life of Wesley and the Rise and Progress of Methodism.* 1820; reprint ed., London: George Bell, 1901. Original edition in two volumes. The first really non-Methodist biography; documented, but with errors of fact and judgment. Essential reading, if for no other reason that to observe Southey's biographical method and style.

Telford, John. *The Life of John Wesley.* London: Hodder and Stoughton, 1886. Written in the same manner as his biography of Charles Wesley, although one wishes for an index.

Tyerman, Luke. *The Life and Times of the Rev. John Wesley, M.A.* 3 vols. 1870; reprint ed., New York: Harper, 1872. Still ranks high for its concreteness and comprehensiveness, although it suffers from Tyerman's enthusiasm for Methodism and his antagonism toward Wesley's opponents.

Vulliamy, Colwyn E. *John Wesley.* London: Geoffrey Bles, 1931. 3d ed. London: Epworth Press, 1954. Valuable not only as a biography, but as a history of the early years of British evangelicalism. Contains a number of sketches of Wesley's supporters, immediate subordinates, and close friends.

Whitehead, John. *The Life of Rev. John Wesley.* 2 vols. London: Stephen Couchman, 1793–1796. Composed during the heat of the debates over the future of British Methodism that followed John Wesley's death. Thus the work functions as an instrument of Whitehead's political persuasions, rather than as an attempt at accurate biography.

Wilson, Thomas Woodrow. *John Wesley's Place in History.* New York: Abingdon Press, 1916. The address delivered by Wilson when, as President of Princeton, he spoke at Wesleyan University (1903) on the occasion of the Wesley bicentennial. Wilson places Wesley in his proper social and economic setting.

Winchester, Caleb Thomas. *John Wesley.* New York: Macmillan, 1906. Valuable for its emphasis upon Wesley and the so-called "great middle-class of English people," whom the author believes Wesley knew better than all of the eighteenth-century *literati* (especially the novelists) combined.

B. Articles

Andrews, Stuart. "John Wesley and the Age of Reason." *History Today* 19 (1969):25–32.

Baker, Frank. "John Wesley and the *Imitatio Christi.*" *London Quarterly and Holborn Review* 165 (January 1941):74–87.

Barber, F. Louis. "John Wesley Edits a Novel." *London Quarterly and Holborn Review* 171 (1946):50–54. Concerns Henry Brooke's *The Fool of Quality* (1760–1772).

Belshaw, Harry. "The Influence of John Wesley on Dr. Johnson's Religion." *London Quarterly and Holborn Review* 167 (July 1943):226–34.

Bett, Henry. "John Wesley's Translations of German Hymns in Reference to Metre and Rhyme." *London Quarterly and Holborn Review* 164 (July 1940):288–94.

Bishop, John. "John Wesley As a Preacher." *Religion in Life* 26 (1957):264–73.

Bowmer, John C. "Dr. Johnson and John Wesley." *New Rambler* 8 (January 1970):12–25.

Brantley, Richard E. "Johnson's Wesleyan Connection." *Eighteenth-Century Studies* 10 (1976–1977):143–68. A thorough but not always convincing argument that strains of Wesleyanism flowed through Johnson's veins.

Brash, W. Bardsley. "Wesley's Wit and Humour." *London Quarterly Review* 135 (January 1921):53–67.

Duncan, Ivar L. "John Wesley Edits *Paradise Lost.*" In: *Essays in Memory of Christine Burleson.* Edited by Thomas G. Barton. Johnson City: East Tennessee State University, 1969, pp. 73–85.

Gillies, Andrew. "Sidelights on John Wesley from Boswell's *Johnson.*" *Methodist Review* 103 (January-February 1920):22–29.

Gleckner, Robert F. "Blake and Wesley." *Notes and Queries* 201 (1956):522–24.

Golden, James L. "John Wesley on Rhetoric and Belles Lettres." *Speech Monographs* 28 (November 1961):250–64.

Harrison, Frank Mott. "Two Johns: Bunyan (1628–1688)—Wesley (1703–1791)." *London Quarterly and Holborn Review* 163 (July 1939):347–54.

Hatfield, James Taft. "John Wesley's Translations of German Hymns." *PMLA* 11 (1896):171–99.

Havens, Raymond D. "Southey's Revision of His *Life of Wesley.*" *Review of English Studies* 22 (1946):134–36.

Keynes, Sir Geoffrey. "Blake and Wesley." *Notes and Queries* 202 (1957):181.

Kuhn, A. J. "Nature Spiritualized: Aspects of Anti-Newtonianism." *English Literary History* 41 (1974):400–412. Value over fact and grace over nature, as seen in the writings of Byrom, Law, John Wesley, and Hervey.

Leach, Elsie A. "John Wesley's Use of George Herbert." *Huntington Library Quarterly* 16 (1953):183–202.

Lidgett, J. S. "John Wesley and John Henry Newman." *London Quarterly Review* 146 (1926):1–10.

Lyles, Albert M. "The Hostile Reaction to the American Views of Johnson and Wesley." *Journal of the Rutgers University Library* 24 (1960):1–13. Concerns Wesley's *Calm Address to Our American Colonies.*

Malekin, Peter. "William Law and John Wesley." *Studia Neophilologica* 37 (1965):190–98. Concerns the significance of Law's relationship with Wesley—from Law's point of view.

Mims, E. "John Wesley and Dr. Johnson." *Methodist Review* 63 (1903):543.

Pellowe, John R. "John Wesley's Use of the Bible." *Methodist Review* 106 (May 1923):353–74.

Playter, G.F. "John Wesley As a Man of Literature." *Methodist Quarterly* 18 (1858):272; 19 (1859):548; 20 (1860):260, 264.

Rogal, Samuel J. "John Wesley and the Attack on Luxury in England." *Eighteenth-Century Life* 3 (1977):91–94.

———. "John Wesley on War and Peace." In: *Studies in Eighteenth-Century Culture*. Edited by Roseann Runte. Madison: University of Wisconsin Press, 1978.

———. "John Wesley's Daily Routine." *Methodist History* 13 (October 1974):41–50.

———. "John Wesley's London." *Asbury Seminarian* 34 (January 1979):23–33.

———. "John Wesley's Women." *Eighteenth-Century Life* 1 (October 1974):9–10.

———. "A Journal and Diary Checklist of John Wesley's Reading: 14 October 1735–23 February 1791." *Serif* 11 (1974):11–33.

———. "Kingswood School: John Wesley's Educational Experiment." *Illinois Quarterly* 40 (Summer 1978):5–16.

———. "Pills for the Poor: John Wesley's *Primitive Physick*." *Yale Journal of Biology and Medicine* 51 (1978):81–90.

———. "Scriptural Quotation in Wesley's *Earnest Appeal*." *Research Studies* 47 (September 1979):181–88.

Schofield, Robert E. "John Wesley and Science in Eighteenth-Century England." *Isis* 44 (1953):331–40.

Shepherd, Thomas Boswell. "John Wesley and Matthew Prior." *London Quarterly and Holborn Review* 161 (July 1937):368–73.

Sherwin, Oscar. "Milton for the Masses: John Wesley's Edition of *Paradise Lost*." *Modern Language Quarterly* 12 (1951):267–85.

Smith, Neil G. "The Literary Taste of John Wesley." *Queen's Quarterly* 45 (1938):353–58.

Williamson, Karina. "Herbert's Reputation in the Eighteenth Century." *Philological Quarterly* 41 (October 1962):769–75. Concerns Wesley's "mutilation" of Herbert's poems.

Wright, Louis B. "John Wesley: Scholar and Critic." *South Atlantic Quarterly* 29 (1930):262–81.

C. Dissertations

Cascio, Robert J. "Mystic and Augustan: A Study of the Impact of William Law on John Wesley, Edward Gibbon, and John Byrom." *DAI* 35 (1974):1615A–1616A (Fordham).

Dygoski, Louise Annie. *The Journals and Letters of John Wesley on Preaching*. 1961 (Wisconsin).

Hansen, William A. "John Wesley and the Rhetoric of Reform." *DAI* 33 (1972):843A (Oregon).

Molin, Sven Eric. *John Wesley's Technique in Revising Literary Masterpieces for His Methodist Audience, with Special Reference to PARADISE LOST.* 1956 (Pennsylvania).

Whited, Harold V. *A Rhetorical Analysis of the Published Sermons Preached by John Wesley at Oxford University.* 1959 (Michigan).

Index

173